Contents

6 Foreword
8 Introduction
22 Fashion shops
64 Shoe shops
68 Jewellery shops
78 A shop for spectacles
80 Beauty salons
90 A pipe shop
94 Bookshops
106 Pharmacies
110 A display room for paints
112 A shop for toys and kindergarten equipment
114 Shops for furnishing requisites and furniture
128 Food shops
140 Travel agencies
147 Architects

Inhalt

7 Vorwort
8 Einführung
22 Modegeschäfte
64 Schuhgeschäfte
68 Juweliergeschäfte
78 Ein Geschäft für Brillen
80 Schönheitssalons
90 Ein »Pfeifenarchiv«
94 Buchhandlungen
106 Apotheken
110 Ein Ausstellungsraum für Farben
112 Ein Geschäft für Spielzeug und Kindergartenbedarf
114 Geschäfte für Einrichtungsbedarf und Möbel
128 Lebensmittelgeschäfte
140 Reisebüros
147 Architekten

Foreword

When Gerd Hatje first asked us to do a book on shop design, or to be more precise, a book which, based on about 50 examples, would indicate the problems presented in the design and construction of shops, and at the same time would illustrate allied tendencies in architectural design, we were tempted to refuse. It is extremely difficult, almost impossible even, for architects who are actively engaged in their profession to analyse all the tendencies that exist in present-day architecture. However, shop design in particular clearly reflects the developments of architecture; as a result of the low volume of building and short completion deadlines, new concepts in this sphere become apparent very early. Today these developments are so complex, so equivocal, that even to the attentive observer of the architectural scene the personal stamp of the designer is more familiar than the actual, encompassing "style".
Nevertheless, after due consideration we came to the conclusion that because of our 25 years of experience in shop design and our long-standing interest in the history of architecture, it would be possible to select from among the many projects successfully realized ones which could be relevant to the further development of shop design, and to contemporary architecture in general.
Drawings and photographs in particular convey an impression of the selected shops – in as far as this is possible in two-dimensional representation. In compiling the written descriptions, we seized every opportunity to include the designers' personal interpretations of their work. Where written concepts did not exist, we ventured to reconstruct their idea and design procedures on the basis of the material available.
We have attempted to show a very comprehensive picture of shop design in its present form. If significant examples from recent years have been omitted, it is solely because we were unable to look at the individual shops personally or, for reasons inexplicable to us, no reference was made to them in the professional literature.
We wish to thank Gerd Hatje and his staff for the conscientious effort they have devoted to this book. In our own office, our thanks are directed first and foremost to Frau Genetheim and Frau Nießl who, in addition to the daily office routine, still somehow managed to devote time to the book.
Last but not least, wo would thank all our colleages for placing the material punctually and – in most cases – with detailed documentation at our disposal.

Karl and Eva Mang

NEW SHOPS

Translation into English by Patricia Noris

First published in the U.S.A. 1982
by Architectural Book Publishing Co., Inc.
© 1981 Verlag Gerd Hatje, D-7000 Stuttgart 50, Germany

Library of Congress Cataloging in Publication Data

Mang, Karl, 1922 –
  New shops.

  First published under title: Neue Läden.
  English and German.
  Includes Index.
  1. Stores, Retail–Designs and plans.
2. Architecture, Modern–20th century–Designs and
plans. I. Mang, Eva. II. Title.
NA6220.M2713 1982   725'.21'0904 · 81-14965
ISBN 8038-9525-9   AACR2

Printed in Germany

NEW SHOPS

KARL AND EVA MANG

Architectural Book Publishing Company
New York 10016

Vorwort

Als uns Gerd Hatje aufforderte, ein Buch über Ladenbau zu machen oder, um es genauer zu sagen, ein Buch, das anhand von etwa 50 Beispielen die Probleme beim Entwurf und Bau von Läden, aber auch die Tendenzen architektonischer Gestaltung aufzeigt, war unsere erste Reaktion darauf eher abweisend. Für schaffende Architekten ist es außerordentlich schwierig, ja fast unmöglich, sich mit allen Tendenzen der heutigen Architektur auseinanderzusetzen. Gerade im Ladenbau aber spiegelt sich die Entwicklung der Architektur besonders deutlich – sehr früh werden dort infolge des geringen Bauvolumens und kurzfristiger Realisierungen neue Überlegungen erkennbar –, und diese Entwicklung ist heute mehr denn je so vielschichtig, ja vieldeutig, daß auch für den aufmerksamen Betrachter die Architekturszene eher noch persönliche Handschriften der Gestalter als »Stilrichtungen« sichtbar werden.

Nach reiflicher Überlegung sagten wir uns allerdings, daß unsere 25jährige Erfahrung im Ladenbau und ein langjähriges Interesse für die Geschichte der Architektur es doch möglich machen müßten, aus den vielen Beispielen gelungener Realisierungen jene herauszufinden, die für die weitere Entwicklung des Ladenbaus wie auch des Architekturgeschehens im allgemeinen von Wichtigkeit sein könnten.

Zeichnungen und vor allem Photographien sollen einen Eindruck von den ausgewählten Läden vermitteln – soweit dies bei der zweidimensionalen Darstellungsweise überhaupt möglich ist. Was die verbale Beschreibung betrifft, erschien es uns notwendig und wünschenswert, hier möglichst viel von der eigenen Interpretation der Gestalter einfließen zu lassen. Wo schriftliche Überlegungen zu den Entwürfen nicht vorhanden waren, haben wir das Wagnis unternommen, aus den Unterlagen Idee und Entwurfsvorgang zu rekonstruieren.

Wir haben versucht, ein möglichst breites Bild der heutigen Ladenbauszene zu zeichnen. Wenn wesentliche Beispiele der letzten Jahre nicht behandelt wurden, liegt dies ausschließlich daran, daß wir entweder keine Gelegenheit hatten, die Läden selbst zu sehen, oder diese in der Fachliteratur aus uns nicht bekannten Gründen keine Erwähnung fanden.

Gerd Hatje und seinen Mitarbeitern danken wir für all die Sorgfalt, die sie dem Buch angedeihen ließen. Aus unserem Büro danken wir in erster Linie Frau Genetheim und Frau Nießl, für die es nicht leicht war, neben dem Tagesgeschäft auch noch die Zeit für die Bearbeitung des Buchs zu finden.

Nicht zuletzt dürfen wir allen Kollegen dafür danken, daß sie das Material zeitgerecht und – zumeist – ausführlich dokumentiert zur Verfügung stellten.

Karl und Eva Mang

1. "Floating Market", Bangkok.

1. »Floating Market«, Bangkok.

2. Egyptian tradeswomen, Thebes,
1580–1100 B. C.

2. Ägyptische Händlerinnen, Theben,
1580–1100 v. Chr.

Introduction

Leaving out of account that throughout the ages travelling merchants have carried their wares from market to market, the sale of goods presupposes an appropriate setting, a "place of activity", generally a permanent room. And this setting – the shop, the department store – reflects, despite its fairly trivial function, the cultural niveau of a society. (To what extent our lives are influenced by sales activity can be ascertained from the term "consumer society" which is derived from this same activity.)

The interior arrangement and equipment of a shop are strongly influenced by the designer's explanation of the psychological and technical aspects of sales procedure, and this, in the long run, underlies the developments of architecture in general. The main responsibility for today's large-scale projects, such as department stores, shopping centres or discount stores, is carried by psychologists, business advisors and rationalization experts, and in view of the risks incurred by any large concern in the reorganization of its salesrooms, this may well be justified. The numerous factors which influence decisions, as well as the large group of persons responsible, almost automatically restrict the scope of experiment in design, and this, in turn, virtually rule out individual accomplishments in this field.

The designer of the small shop, on the other hand, has personal contact with the owner himself who, even today, is still receptive to experiments. A close study of the history of shop design reveals that – as in other branches of architecture – the best results are achieved through the congenial cooperation between an understanding and open-minded client and an enterprising architect. That the spatial concepts evolved in this process frequently find their way into mass production by shop design contractors, or are adapted by department store concerns, is almost a matter of course: successful examples are prone to be copied.

We are not questioning the necessity of large organizations: the supply of goods to today's consumer society, a mass society, calls for sales techniques which must, under all circumstances, satisfy the demand, and this huge task cannot be undertaken by the small shop alone.

Whether with scientific consistency or simple intuition, both the furnishing specialists of large companies as well as the designers of small shops do nothing more than create the setting for one of man's oldest activities: namely the exchange, the transaction or the sale of goods.

All over the world we still find people living on the periphery of the civilized world, whose trading activities are deeply rooted in ancient traditions. To the Indian cloth seller, the shopkeeper in an Arabian souk or the fruit vendor in the "Floating Market" in Bangkok, the delivery, storage and display of goods as well as their protection from the elements (in other words, all aspects of "sales organization" in the broadest sense of the word), are a matter of routine. A naive understanding of human nature gives them the same self-assurance in sales talk as the university training of the sales director of a large western concern. Only by "selling" goods as a means of earning their livelihood can they both prove the necessity of their action. Selling is thus synonymous with the establishment of a goods/customer relationship – in Egypt four thousand years ago just as in London's Bond Street today – and necessitates in most cases a properly designed enclosure.

Throughout the ages, advantage has been taken of the latest devices, whether of an architectural or technical nature, to create an appropriate setting for showing the merchandise to the customer. Although now in ruins, the market hall at the Forum of Trajan in Rome has retained its fascination by virtue of its obvious efficiency, spaciousness and order. In its formal and technical splendour as well as in the high quality of the materials used it was by no means inferior to the 19th century American department store.

The market stalls of the medieval town, whose wooden frames with their sunproof or rainproof cloth coverings could be quickly dismantled, were very similar in construction to the stands which still dominate the scene today at the weekly markets in those towns where this tradition has been retained. The daily food market in a covered, sheltered hall

Einführung

Der Verkauf von Waren benötigt einen Rahmen, einen »Ort der Handlung«, einen üblicherweise ortsgebundenen Raum, sehen wir einmal davon ab, daß es zu allen Zeiten von Markt zu Markt ziehende Händler gegeben hat. Und an diesem Rahmen, dem Laden, dem Kaufhaus, kann trotz seiner recht profanen Aufgabe über den Fortschritt technischer Einrichtungen hinaus nichts weniger als der jeweilige Stand der Kultur einer Gesellschaft abgelesen werden. (Wie bestimmend die Tätigkeit des Verkaufens für unser heutiges Leben ist, sehen wir daran, daß der Begriff der »Konsumgesellschaft« eben von dieser Tätigkeit abgeleitet wurde.)

Raum und Ausstattung eines Ladens werden von der Auseinandersetzung des Gestalters mit der Psychologie und Technik des Verkaufs geprägt, einer Auseinandersetzung, die nicht zuletzt von der Entwicklung der Architektur im allgemeinen abhängig ist. Bei Großprojekten unserer Zeit, etwa bei Kaufhäusern, Einkaufszentren oder Billigmärkten, liegt der Schwerpunkt der Verantwortlichkeit ohne Zweifel bei Psychologen, Betriebsberatern und Rationalisierungsfachleuten, und dies mag bei dem Risiko, das ein großes Unternehmen bei der Neugestaltung seiner Verkaufsräume eingeht, berechtigt sein. Die Vielzahl der Faktoren für die Entscheidungsfindung sowie der große Kreis verantwortlicher Personen engen fast automatisch die Möglichkeit des Experiments in Fragen der Gestaltung ein, ein Grund mehr dafür, daß selbständige Leistungen in diesem Bereich nur selten erwartet werden können.

Dagegen bleibt der kleine Laden, bei dessen Gestaltung der Entwerfer der persönliche Gesprächspartner des Inhabers ist, auch heute noch dem Experiment aufgeschlossen. Befaßt man sich näher mit der Geschichte des Ladenbaus, kann man – wie auch sonst in der Architektur – feststellen, daß die besten Beispiele nahezu immer in kongenialer Zusammenarbeit eines verständnisvollen und aufgeschlossenen Bauherrn und eines wagemutigen Architekten entstehen. Daß die hierbei gefundenen Raumkonzeptionen häufig den Weg in die Serie der Ladenbaufirmen finden oder von Kaufhauskonzernen übernommen werden, ist fast selbstverständlich: Erfolgreiche Beispiele werden nur zu gern nachgeahmt.

Es soll hier nicht die Notwendigkeit der Großorganisation in Zweifel gezogen werden: Die Versorgung der heutigen Konsumgesellschaft, einer Gesellschaft der Masse, verlangt nach Verkaufsformen, die, unter welchen Bedingungen auch immer, den Bedarf befriedigen, und das kann nicht allein durch den kleinen Laden geschehen.

3. Market hall at the Forum of Trajan, Rome.

3. Markthalle am Trajansforum, Rom.

4. Market in San Gimignano.

4. Markt in San Gimignano.

5. Food shop in Pompeii.

5. Eßwarenladen in Pompeji.

on the main square of San Gimignano, like the small shops which line the narrow streets of the Arabian souks, demonstrates a sales technique which is ageless and which, as far as the intensity of the sales pitch is concerned, far outmatches the sales potential of a modern department store.

The formal appearance of the small shop, which can be traced back, as a type at least, to Ancient Rome and which has dominated the scene in the main streets and squares of our towns since the late Middle Ages, has always been influenced by the evolution of architecture. The shape and construction of the shop front alone usually disclose its year of origin – as does the use of technical devices available. The size of the shop-window, of the glazed surface, is determined by the technical means available, though often, for traditional reasons – as in England – the small sash bar division has been retained. For centuries, however, the door provided the only opening onto the street for many of the smaller shops, such as the bakery shop or the cobbler's shop, which were usually situated on the ground floor of the shopkeeper's own house. In the evening this door was closed with shutters. This type of shop still exists today in the small alleys of many old towns.

The quality of the construction and furnishings obviously depended on the "status" of the shop, on its clientèle, its location in the town, and the quality of merchandise. The furnishings of many earlier shops were traditionally of a very high quality, a characteristic which is still apparent in old, well-preserved pharmacies whose excellent joinery work easily competes with the elaborate receptacles for ointments and medicines. Exploiting the health of our fellowmen for business reasons has probably never been unprofitable.

The 19th century, which was accompanied by rapidly expanding towns and intensive new building activity in the old town centres also, made new demands on shop design. Constructions were developed for the large tenement blocks which made serial production possible and necessary. The ground-floor fronts of the houses in the Linke Wienzeile, designed by Otto Wagner and completed in 1898, have remained unaltered in detail: wood construction, large shop-windows to enhance display, slatted roller blinds to protect the shop – and lettering was the only break in uniformity.

Shopping galleries represent a special form of 19th century shop design. To make shopping possible in all kinds of weather, wide interior spaces, accessible from main shopping streets and illuminated from above by means of iron and glass constructions, were developed in courts built especially for this purpose. A typical example of the latter, in particular with regard to the general uniformity of the shop fronts and the strict

Sowohl die Einrichtungsfachleute der großen Unternehmen als auch die Gestalter der kleinen Läden tun nichts anderes, als mit wissenschaftlicher Konsequenz oder rein intuitiv den Rahmen für eine der ältesten Tätigkeiten des Menschen zu schaffen: nämlich die des Tauschs, des Handels oder des Verkaufs von Waren.

Wer heute durch die Welt reist, kann, am Rande der Zivilisation, immer noch Menschen treffen, deren Handelstätigkeit zutiefst in uralten Traditionen verhaftet ist. Ein indischer Stoffverkäufer, der Inhaber eines Ladens in einem arabischen Souk oder ein Obstverkäufer im »Floating Market« in Bangkok beherrscht mit großer Selbstverständlichkeit all die Dinge, die wir mit »Verkaufsorganisation« im weitesten Sinn des Worts umschreiben können, wie etwa den Antransport, die Lagerung und die Schaustellung der Waren sowie deren Schutz vor der Witterung. Eine naive Menschenkenntnis gibt ihnen dieselbe Sicherheit im Verkaufsgespräch wie das Studium an einer Hochschule dem Verkaufsdirektor eines westlichen Großkonzerns. Beide können eben nur dann die Notwendigkeit ihres Handelns beweisen, wenn sie Ware »verkaufen« und durch diese Tätigkeit ihren Lebensunterhalt verdienen. Verkaufen also heißt, die Beziehung Ware – Kunde herzustellen, vor viertausend Jahren in Ägypten ebenso wie in Londons Bond Street von heute – und dazu bedarf es in den allermeisten Fällen eines gestalteten Raums.

Das Zusammentreffen von Kunde und Ware hat zu jeder Zeit die neuesten Errungenschaften benutzt, um sich seinen Rahmen zu schaffen, sei es in architektonischer oder in technischer Hinsicht. Noch heute besticht die Ruine der Markthalle am Trajansforum in Rom durch augenscheinliche Funktionstüchtigkeit, Großzügigkeit und Ordnung. In ihrer formalen, technischen wie auch materialmäßigen Pracht stand sie einem amerikanischen Warenhaus des 19. Jahrhunderts sicherlich in keiner Weise nach.

Den Marktbuden einer mittelalterlichen Stadt, deren Holzgestelle mit Sonnen- oder Regenschutz aus Stoff in kurzer Zeit demontiert werden konnten, gleichen in ihrer Konstruktion noch heute die Stände, die die Wochenmärkte jener Städte beherrschen, die sich diese Einrichtung zu bewahren wußten. Der tägliche Lebensmittelmarkt in einer überdeckten und dadurch geschützten Halle am Hauptplatz von San Gimignano ist ebenso Beispiel zeitloser Verkaufstechnik wie die aneinandergereihten kleinen Läden in den Gassen der arabischen Souks, die, von der Intensität des Verkaufsgesprächs aus gesehen, die Verkaufsmöglichkeiten eines modernen Warenhauses weit überragen.

Der kleine Laden, zumindest als Typ schon in der römischen Antike nachweisbar und bestimmend für das Bild der Hauptstraßen und Plätze unserer Städte seit dem späten Mittelalter, war von der formalen Gestaltung her immer besonders eng mit der Entwicklung der Architektur verbunden. Schon aus der Form und Konstruktion der Schaufensterfront ist meist das Entstehungsjahr ablesbar – ebenso aus dem Einsatz bereits verfügbarer technischer Mittel. Die Größe der Schaufenster und damit der

6. Closed shops in the old part of Prague.

6. Verschlossene Läden in der Prager Altstadt.

7. Pharmacy "zur Madonna", Bozen (Bolzano), 1897.

7. Apotheke zur Madonna, Bozen, 1897.

8. Houses in the Linke Wienzeile, Vienna, 1898. Otto Wagner.

8. Häuser an der Linken Wienzeile, Wien, 1898. Otto Wagner.

regulation in detail, is the Burlington Arcade in London. Galleries of this type sprang up in almost every European city, only to give way later to department stores. Their technical and architectural influence, however, is not only apparent in shop design; the basic principle, namely the concentration of a variety of small shops, is being widely adopted again today in town centre rehabilitation programmes – the Calwer Passage in Stuttgart is a typical example.

Shop design already played a considerable role in the initial attempts to overcome Historicism in architecture. Buildings such as Victor Horta's A l'Innovation department store in Brussels, Henry van de Velde's shop for the Habana-Compagnie in Berlin, and August Endell's Elvira photographic studio in Munich were individual solutions which pioneered subsequent developments. They were signals, visions, events; and their influence on architectural design extended far beyond the mere realization of the building projects in question. The experimentation with new forms not only contributed to the enrichment of the façades, but also, and above all, to the enhancement of interior design. To what extent shop design can influence architecture in general is demonstrated by Adolf Loos. His early work in Vienna made his hostility towards ornamentation, his advocation of the appropriate use of materials and his striving for consistency in spatial design just as much well-known as did his work in the field of domestic architecture. Whether the Kniže men's fashion shop or the Goldman & Salatsch men's fashion shop in the building on the Michaelerplatz – where for the first time he was able to realize the "room plan" which greatly influenced the development of modern architecture –, these small projects in particular offered Loos the possibility of experimentation. The influence of the interior design of the American Bar in the Kärntner Durchgang, or the axial solution of the Kniže men's fashion shop is still apparent in Vienna's shop architecture today.

With regard to Otto Wagner, reference must be made to the rows of shops on the ground floor of his tenement houses – from those which originated during the time of Historicism to those constructed in 1909 in the tenement block in the Neustiftgasse. Additionally significant are the individual works of this distinguished Viennese master, such as his Die Zeit telegraph office, where aluminium, then a new material, was employed with great success.

The twenties and thirties brought especially strong impetuses to architecture in general and to shop design in particular. In Holland, Gerrit Thomas Rietveld built his shops

Glasflächen richtet sich nach den technischen Möglichkeiten, wenn auch oft aus Tradition – etwa in England – die kleine Sprossenteilung bis in unsere Zeit bestehen blieb. Der einfache Laden allerdings, die Bäckerei, die Schuhmacherei, zumeist im Erdgeschoß des eigenen Wohnhauses untergebracht, öffnete sich über Jahrhunderte zur Straße lediglich mit der Tür, des Abends mit Läden verschließbar, was sich bis heute in manchen kleinen Gäßchen alter Städte erhalten hat.

Die Qualität der Konstruktion und Einrichtung blieb selbstverständlich abhängig vom »Status« des Ladens, also von seiner Kundschaft, der Lage in der Stadt und der Güte der Waren. Gerade viele frühere Läden wiesen in der Einrichtung eine – durch Tradition herausgebildete – hohe Qualität auf, was besonders die noch erhaltenen alten Apotheken zeigen, deren großartige Tischlerarbeiten mit den kunstvollen Behältern für Salben und Medikamente konkurrieren. Das Geschäft mit der Gesundheit der Mitmenschen dürfte zu keiner Zeit das schlechteste gewesen sein.

Das 19. Jahrhundert, das ein rasches Wachsen der Stadt und eine intensive Neubautätigkeit auch in alten Stadtkernen brachte, stellte ganz neue Anforderungen an den Ladenbau. Für die großen Mietskasernen entstanden Konstruktionen, die eine serielle Herstellung möglich und notwendig machten. Otto Wagners 1898 entstandene Häuser an der Linken Wienzeile weisen noch heute im gesamten Straßengeschoß die gleichen Fassadendetails auf: Holzkonstruktion, große Scheiben für die Auslagen, Rollbalken zum Schutz des Ladens – die Uniformität wurde lediglich durch die Beschriftung unterbrochen.

Eine Sonderform der Ladengestaltung im 19. Jahrhundert stellen die Läden in den Passagen dar. Von Hauptgeschäftsstraßen aus zugänglich, entstanden in den dafür

9. Burlington Arcade, London, 1815–19.
10. Calwer Passage, Stuttgart. Kammerer + Belz und Partner.

13. Elvira photographic studio, Munich, 1897/8.
August Endell.

13. Photoatelier Elvira, München, 1897/98.
August Endell.

11. A l'Innovation department store, Brussels,
1901. Victor Horta.
12. Shop for the Habana-Compagnie, Berlin,
1899. Henry van de Velde.

11. Kaufhaus A l'Innovation, Brüssel, 1901.
Victor Horta.
12. Laden der Habana-Compagnie, Berlin, 1899.
Henry van de Velde.

designed in the constructivistic manner of the De Stijl group, while in Germany, Herbert Bayer's Bauhaus designs for shops and sales kiosks were the topic of discussion. Le Corbusier's concept for shops of the Bat'a shoe company, which unfortunately remained unrealized, demonstrated the possibilities of standard elements (for the exterior form as well as for the interior) for a world-wide chain of shops. Arne Jacobsen also ventured into the field of shop design – the kiosk shown here was built by him in 1932 on the Bellevue bathing beach near Copenhagen.

After World War II, modern architecture was able to assert itself on a wide basis; however, its misconceived application in the mass production of huge shop-window constructions soon led to the destruction of the grown structure of whole rows of streets. This was particularly tragic in towns where the building substance had hardly been affected by the war. In spite of the cosmopolitan nature of modern architecture, regional differences soon became apparent. While in Central Europe (Germany and Austria) the existing building substance of the ground floor was being broken up (by "removal of piers"), Paris, Milan and Rome were paying heed to the existing architecture – particularly in the more important shopping streets. Here, the attempt was being made to conform to the structure of the entire façade.

The examples selected for this book originated in the last 10 years. During this time, architecture experienced the transition from the International Style to "post-modern" architecture, which rejects the ideas of the Bauhaus and its successors and attempts to counter these with the introduction of a new architectural "language". These tendencies are also perceptible in shop design and will be dealt with later by means of the examples. A further significant prerequisite for the change in shop design emerged from the economic recession resulting from the energy crisis and, in this connection, from calling the consumer society into question. Even in the sixties, the experts were still emphasizing the necessity of renewing furnishings and shop fronts every 7 to 10 years as a consequence of world-wide economic activity. There can hardly be any question of that today. In shop design, on the one hand, emphasis is being placed on quality and durability, while on the other hand, the young people in particular want the "simple" shop, the shop which is neither perfect nor "permanent", which changes in order to stay young.

The work of the Japanese architect Shiro Kuramata is typical of the designs which originated in the late phase of the International Style. They excel by virtue of precision in detail and a spatial significance which is related to the tradition of the Japanese house. Spatial order, an "emptiness" hardly conceivable in a sales establishment, and colouring

14. Kniže men's fashion shop, Vienna, 1909–13.
Adolf Loos.
15. Goldman & Salatsch men's fashion shop in
the building on the Michaelerplatz, Vienna,
1910/1. Adolf Loos.

14. Herrenmodegeschäft Kniže, Wien, 1909–13.
Adolf Loos.
15. Herrenmodegeschäft Goldman & Salatsch im
Haus am Michaelerplatz, Wien, 1910/11.
Adolf Loos.

gebauten Höfen weite, von oben über Eisen- und Glaskonstruktionen beleuchtete Innenräume, die ein wettergeschütztes Einkaufen ermöglichen. Ein typisches Beispiel, besonders auch im Hinblick auf die zumeist gleichförmigen Schaufensterfronten und das strenge Reglement für die Detailausbildung, ist die Burlington Arcade in London. Fast in allen europäischen Städten entstanden derartige Passagen, die später den Kaufhäusern wichen. In Technik und Architektur haben sie sicherlich nicht nur den Ladenbau beeinflußt. In der Altstadtsanierung von heute wird dieses Prinzip des konzentrierten Angebots kleiner Geschäfte wieder aufgenommen – als Beispiel mag die Calwer Passage in Stuttgart gelten.

Schon an den ersten Versuchen, den Historismus in der Architektur zu überwinden, war der Ladenbau maßgeblich beteiligt. Bauten wie Victor Hortas Kaufhaus A l'Innovation in Brüssel, Henry van de Veldes Laden der Habana-Compagnie in Berlin und August Endells Photoatelier Elvira in München haben als Einzellösungen bahnbrechend gewirkt. Es waren Fanale, Visionen, Ereignisse, die weit über die bescheidenen Bauaufgaben hinaus die architektonische Gestaltung beeinflußten. Das Spiel mit neuen Formen bereicherte nicht nur die Fassaden, sondern vor allem auch die Innenarchitektur in entscheidender Weise. Wie weit der Einfluß des Ladenbaus auf die Architektur im allgemeinen gehen kann, zeigt Adolf Loos. Seine frühen Arbeiten in der Wiener Innenstadt machten seine Architekturphilosophie der Ornamentlosigkeit, sein Bekenntnis zur Materialgerechtigkeit und sein Bemühen um konsequent gestaltete Räume ebenso bekannt wie seine Arbeiten im Wohnbereich. Gerade diese kleinen Bauaufgaben gaben Loos die Möglichkeit zum Experiment, ob es sich nun um das Herrenmodegeschäft Kniže oder das Herrenmodegeschäft Goldman & Salatsch im Haus am Michaelerplatz handelte, wo er übrigens erstmals seinen für die Entwicklung der modernen Architektur so wesentlichen »Raumplan« realisieren konnte. Der Innenraum der American Bar im Kärntner Durchgang oder die axiale Lösung des Herrenmodegeschäfts Kniže wirken auf die Ladenbauarchitektur in Wien bis heute nach.

Bei Otto Wagner sind es vor allem die Ladenreihen im Erdgeschoß seiner Mietshäuser, die hier genannt werden müssen – von den frühen aus der Zeit des Historismus bis hin zu denen im Mietshaus in der Neustiftgasse aus dem Jahr 1909. Der Wiener Meister ist daneben jedoch auch mit Einzelarbeiten hervorgetreten, etwa mit dem Depeschenbüro Die Zeit, bei dem das neue Material Aluminium in überzeugender Weise angewendet wurde.

In den zwanziger und dreißiger Jahren erhielt nicht nur die Architektur im allgemeinen, sondern auch der Ladenbau besonders starke neue Impulse. In Holland entstanden die im Konstruktivismus der Stijlgruppe gehaltenen Läden von Gerrit Thomas Rietveld, und in Deutschland machten die am Bauhaus entstandenen Entwürfe für Läden und Verkaufskioske von Herbert Bayer von sich reden. Le Corbusiers leider nicht realisierte Konzeption für Läden des Schuhkonzerns Bat'a zeigte die Möglichkeiten der Gestaltung einer weltumspannenden Ladenkette mit Typenelementen sowohl für die Außenform als auch für den Innenraum auf. Auch Arne Jacobsen hat sich auf dem Gebiet des Ladenbaus versucht – so baute er 1932 im Strandbad von Bellevue bei Kopenhagen den hier gezeigten Kiosk.

Nach dem Zweiten Weltkrieg konnte sich zwar die moderne Architektur auf breiter Basis durchsetzen, bald aber zerstörte deren mißverstandene Anwendung mit der Massenanfertigung riesiger Schaufensterkonstruktionen die gewachsene Ordnung ganzer Straßenzüge. Dies war besonders tragisch in Städten, in denen die Bausubstanz durch den Krieg kaum gelitten hatte. Trotz der Internationalität der Moderne wurden hier bald regionale Unterschiede sichtbar. Während etwa in Mitteleuropa (Deutschland, Österreich) die bestehende Bausubstanz des Erdgeschosses aufgelöst wurde (»Pfeilerentfernung«), nahm man in Paris, Mailand oder Rom – vor allem in den wichtigsten Geschäftsstraßen – Rücksicht auf die bestehende Architektur. Man versuchte hier, sich der Gliederung der Gesamtfassade anzupassen, unterzuordnen.

Die für dieses Buch ausgewählten Beispiele stammen aus den letzten 10 Jahren. In dieser Zeit ging die Architektur den Weg vom Internationalen Stil zur »postmodernen« Architektur, die das Ideengut des Bauhauses und seiner Nachfolger verwirft und versucht,

which is restricted to the simplest elements unite to form a basic principle which distinctly echoes the words of Mies van der Rohe: "Less is more". Further simplification is difficult to imagine.

In diametrical contrast to this conception is the Quantas boutique in Vigo, Spain, by Natalio Arnoso and Diethelm Lenze, which embodies the principle of organized formlessness. Here, the tendency of the youth of today, to see things simply as they are, is the principle element in the design. It is chaos, certainly, but staged with a great deal of charm and feeling, a stage for play, for youth and lightheartedness. Is a greater contrast possible?

Let us include in this context Verena Huber's Hand'art shop in Zurich, which embodies the workshop, the work, the principle of the simply natural, exactly as it is accepted by the youth of today. It is not the design that plays the decisive role here, but the idea to give scope to activity, to create a centre which employs the simplest media to "bring goods to view".

The outset of a concept is very often the wish to create an unmistakable setting. The arguments in favour of the extremely well-known "envelope" for the sale of merchandise are very convincing. Consistency, durability and uniformity are consciously used as means of promotion. The façade thus becomes the "sign" of the space which, for years remaining unchanged, becomes a memorable, almost nostalgic, experience. The First of August fashion shop in New York by George Ranalli is a typical example.

This principle strongly contrasts with the principle of variability, which can also be applied in a small shop. The initial costs in both cases are almost the same, but considerations differ: With a constant basic structure, certain areas of a variable shop can permanently be renewed, altered, or added to, so that they will always attract attention. The principle of the variable shop is as old as the market stall, the flexible construction of which makes every form of display possible. In present-day terms, this means nothing more than placing a "stage construction" at the shop-owner's disposal; with it he can get up his own "sales" performance. However, like a good performance in the theatre, this presupposes a stage-manager. And this is where the difficulties lie: which proprietor of a small shop is prepared to keep planning alterations, or more precisely to supervise the quality of these alterations? Experience has shown that the quality requirements set by the architect often fall short of standard. The idea, however, to employ a technical skeleton similar to a stage construction for the purpose of emphasizing new aspects of sales promotion is very appealing. In this context, reference must be made to the pocket-book department of the Morawa & Co. bookshop in Vienna, where we ourselves were able to realize this concept of a variable shop to a large extent.

The tendencies in the architecture of recent years are — as already mentioned — clearly apparent in shop design. Illusions of space as presented in the Lanvin boutique in Zurich by Robert Haussmann and Trix Haussmann-Högl, where the materials used were also employed as illusionistic agents, would have been inconceivable in the sixties. The interpretation of the language of "post-modern" architecture plays a significant role in the technique of shop design today. With the Pfeifenarchiv in Stuttgart by Peter Haas, Günter Hermann and Werner Schwarz, this principle has been consistently pursued to the end; allusions to the architecture of the past have been brought into play in relation to the functional prerequisites of sales procedure, and materials and forms have been used for the sake of their symbolic value. Hans Hollein is undoubtedly a pioneer of this type of shop design. Charles Jencks, the apostle of "post-modern" architecture, aptly subsumes his perfect creations under the term "consumer temples".

The further development of shop design is closely related to the location. A hig-quality, future-orientated architectural solution presupposes a healthy economic basis, the merchant's faith in positive development in the years to come. A street, a square, a district must offer a promising outlook for the future; only success in business, or the chance of achieving success in the near future gives the merchant the incentive to consent to advertising measures which include the design of the shop. One cannot but admire the courage of the merchant who, under pressure from the large chains of department stores on the one hand, and with his possibilities restricted by the shift in buying activity on the

16. Tenement block in the Neustiftgasse 40, Vienna, 1909. Otto Wagner.

16. Mietshaus Neustiftgasse 40, Wien, 1909. Otto Wagner.

17. Die Zeit telegraph office, Vienna, 1902.
Otto Wagner.

17. Depeschenbüro Die Zeit, Wien, 1902.
Otto Wagner.

18. Shop in the Kalverstraat, Amsterdam,
existing 1922–5. Gerrit Thomas Rietveld.

18. Laden in der Kalverstraat, Amsterdam,
bestand 1922–25. Gerrit Thomas Rietveld.

diesem eine neue Architektur-»Sprache« entgegenzusetzen. Diese Tendenzen sind natürlich auch im Ladenbau zu spüren, worüber anhand der Beispiele noch zu sprechen sein wird.

Eine weitere entscheidende Voraussetzung für den Wandel im Ladenbau ergab sich aus der wirtschaftlichen Rezession als Folge der Energiekrise und der in diesem Zusammenhang stehenden Infragestellung der Konsumgesellschaft. Noch in den sechziger Jahren hielten es die Fachleute im Zeichen einer weltweiten Konjunktur für notwendig, Einrichtung und Schaufensterfront alle 7 bis 10 Jahre zu erneuern. Davon kann heute kaum mehr die Rede sein. Auf der einen Seite steht nun auch in der Ladengestaltung Gediegenheit und Dauerhaftigkeit wieder im Vordergrund, auf der anderen Seite wünscht besonders die Jugend den »einfachen« Laden, den Laden, der weder perfekt noch »endgültig« ist, der sich wandelt, um jung zu bleiben.

Die Arbeiten des Japaners Shiro Kuramata sind beispielhaft für das, was in der Spätphase des Internationalen Stils entstand. Sie zeichnen sich aus durch eine dem Formgefühl des Japaners entsprechende Präzision des Details und eine Bedeutung des Raums, die in gewissem Sinn auf der Tradition des japanischen Hauses fußt. Ordnung, eine für den »Verkauf« kaum mehr zu akzeptierende »Leere« und eine auf einfachste Komponenten reduzierte Farbgebung vereinigen sich zu einem Grundprinzip, das dem Wort »Weniger ist mehr« von Mies van der Rohe auf das deutlichste entspricht. Eine weitere Vereinfachung ist kaum noch denkbar.

Dieser Auffassung diametral gegenüber steht etwa die Boutique Quantas in Vigo, Spanien, von Natalio Arnoso und Diethelm Lenze, die das Prinzip der arrangierten Formlosigkeit verkörpert. Hier spielt die Tendenz der heutigen Jugend, einfach die Dinge so zu sehen, wie sie nun einmal sind, als Gestaltungselement die Hauptrolle. Ein Chaos, ja, aber irgendwie mit viel Charme und Gefühl inszeniert, eine Bühne des Spiels, der Jugend, der Unbekümmertheit. Kann es größere Gegensätze geben?

Nehmen wir dazu noch als Beispiel den Züricher Laden Hand'art von Verena Huber, der die Werkstatt verkörpert, das Arbeiten, das Prinzip des Einfach-Natürlichen, wie es ebenso von der heutigen Jugend akzeptiert wird. Hier ist nicht die »Gestaltung« entscheidend, sondern die Idee, Aktivitäten Raum zu geben, ein Zentrum zu schaffen, das mit einfachen Mitteln Ware »aufzeigt«.

Sehr oft steht der Wunsch, einen unverwechselbaren Rahmen zu schaffen, am Beginn eines Konzepts. Die weithin bekannte »Hülle« für den Verkauf einer Ware hat bestechende Argumente. Konsequenz, Dauerhaftigkeit, Einheitlichkeit werden damit bewußt als Werbemittel eingesetzt. Die Fassade wird damit zum »Zeichen« des über Jahre unveränderten Raums, zum – fast nostalgischen – Erinnerungserlebnis. Ein typisches Beispiel hierfür ist das Modegeschäft First of August in New York von George Ranalli.

Diesem Prinzip steht das der Variabilität gegenüber, die sich auch im kleinen Laden realisieren läßt. Die Anschaffungskosten werden in beiden Fällen etwa in gleicher Höhe liegen, die Überlegung liegt in einem anderen Bereich. Der variable Laden kann immer wieder, bei gleichbleibender Grundstruktur, in bestimmten Bereichen erneuert, geändert, ergänzt werden und so die Aufmerksamkeit erregen. Das Prinzip des veränderlichen Ladens ist so alt wie der Marktstand, dessen flexible Konstruktion jede Art der Darstellung der Ware ermöglicht. In unsere Zeit übersetzt, heißt dies nichts anderes, als dem Eigentümer eine »Bühnenkonstruktion« zur Verfügung zu stellen, mit der er das Schauspiel »Verkauf« inszenieren kann. Allerdings setzt dies, wie eine gute Inszenierung im Theater, einen guten Regisseur voraus. Und hier liegen gerade die Schwierigkeiten: Welcher Inhaber eines kleinen Ladens gibt sich die Mühe, immer wieder Veränderungen zu planen, vor allem die Qualität der Änderungen zu überwachen? Sehr bald werden, wie die Erfahrung zeigt, die vom Architekten gesetzten Qualitätsanforderungen unterschritten. Die Idee allerdings, ein technisches Gerippe ähnlich einer Bühnenkonstruktion einzusetzen, um immer wieder neue Momente der Verkaufswerbung in den Vordergrund zu stellen. hat etwas Bestechendes. Verwiesen sei in diesem Zusammenhang etwa auf die Taschenbuchabteilung der Buchhandlung Morawa & Co. in Wien, bei der wir selbst den Gedanken des variablen Ladens weitgehend realisieren konnten.

Die Tendenzen des Architekturgeschehens der letzten Jahre werden – wie erwähnt – im

19. Concept for shops of the Bat'a shoe company, 1936. Le Corbusier.

19. Konzeption für Läden des Schuhkonzerns Bat'a, 1936. Le Corbusier.

20. Sales kiosk, 1924, project. Herbert Bayer.
21. Kiosk on the Bellevue bathing beach, Copenhagen, 1932. Arne Jacobsen.

20. Verkaufskiosk, 1924, Entwurf. Herbert Bayer.
21. Kiosk im Strandbad Bellevue, Kopenhagen, 1932. Arne Jacobsen.

other, ventures to entrust the design of his shop to a progressive designer. The merchant, in fact, appears to be one of the very few people who are able to appreciate the prospects offered by an unusual design – in this case by a unmistakable shop.

If the population drift continues, the city centre will become more and more like a large museum, and consequently, the shops which place value on quality will move out into the suburbs. A number of the large shopping streets of the 19th century (Merceria in Venice or Kärntner Strasse in Vienna) have already surrendered to mass tourism; quality has been replaced by quantity, famous shops have been replaced by cheap souvenir shops, crammed with merchandise, which only appeal to primitive tastes. Shops of this type are hardly compatible with fastidious building forms, with the uniqueness of bold architectural visions. In the suburbs, where life is increasingly shifting, it is not the quality shop that is in demand but the supermarket, the discount shop, the shopping centre surrounded by hundreds of cars. Here, the only chance of survival for the individual shop is its incorporation into the uniformly-designed complex of one of these centres.

The far-reaching effects of monument preservation are becoming a real problem to the development of a new architectural language in shop design. The preservation of whole areas is undoubtedly a positive measure, though exaggerated demands can have very serious consequences for the building activity of a town. The subsequent outcome of placing whole city centres under a preservation order – as in Vienna – is the migration of vital organisms – first of all the inhabitants themselves, then the organizations and offices and finally the merchants, whether it is the anonymous chain of department stores or the small, self-employed retailer. The tragedy of a purely historicising conception of urban development lies in the foreseeable death of the city centre, in the transformation of whole parts of a city into huge museums which the community, in the long run, will be unable to maintain. Mass tourism is no substitute for pulsating life – the fate of Venice has demonstrated this all too clearly.

The individual shop is also affected by this problem. Its incorporation into a centuries-old façade is conceivable – but how can one expect an architect today to be able to reproduce a rococo porticus for example (whereby the problems of construction, or rather of reproduction, are not solely of a financial nature).

Leaving aside the extent of the work involved, the technique of shop design is identical to that of any other building task. It demands absolute precision from the planning architect during the course of the building work, and above all in the coordination between the contractors who, all too often, are forced to work under cramped conditions. Since the dates of completion are usually already fixed when design work commences – they depend on the start of the sales season, on holiday periods etc. – the length of time allotted for the actual conversion is limited and therefore presupposes very exact planning.

At first this planning is concerned with the purely technical aspects of sales procedure.

22. Issey Miyake boutique, Tokyo. Shiro Kuramata.
23. Quantas boutique, Vigo, Spain. Interplay
(Natalio Arnoso and Diethelm Lenze).
24. Hand'art handicraft shop, Zurich. Verena
Huber.

22. Boutique Issey Miyake, Tokio. Shiro Kuramata.
23. Boutique Quantas, Vigo, Spanien. Interplay
(Natalio Arnoso und Diethelm Lenze).
24. Handarbeitsladen Hand'art, Zürich. Verena
Huber.

Ladenbau deutlich und frühzeitig sichtbar. Raumillusionen, wie etwa bei der Boutique Lanvin in Zürich von Robert Haussmann und Trix Haussmann-Högl, bei der auch das Material illusionistisch eingesetzt wurde, wären noch in den sechziger Jahren undenkbar gewesen. Hier spielt die Übersetzung der Sprache der »postmodernen« Architektur in die Praxis des Ladenbaus von heute eine wesentliche Rolle. Im Pfeifenarchiv in Stuttgart von Peter Haas, Günter Hermann und Werner Schwarz wurde dieses Prinzip dann konsequent zu Ende gedacht; Anspielungen auf die Architektur der Vergangenheit wurden in Beziehung gesetzt zu den funktionalen Bedingungen des Verkaufs, Materialien und Formen um ihres symbolischen Werts willen zur Anwendung gebracht. Ein Pionier dieser Art der Ladengestaltung ist zweifellos Hans Hollein. Charles Jencks, der Apostel der »postmodernen« Architektur, subsumiert seine perfekten Realisationen treffend unter dem Begriff »Tempel des Konsums«.

Die weitere Entwicklung des Ladenbaus steht in einem engen Zusammenhang mit dem Standort. Für eine Lösung mit qualitätsvoller, zukunftsorientierter Architektur bedarf es vor allem einer gesunden wirtschaftlichen Basis, des Glaubens des Geschäftsmanns an eine positive Entwicklung in den nächsten Jahren. Eine Straße, ein Platz, ein Viertel muß zukunftsträchtig erscheinen, nur ein geschäftlicher Erfolg oder die Chance, diesen in naher Zukunft zu erzielen, läßt dem Kaufmann werbliche Maßnahmen, zu denen auch die Gestaltung des Ladens gehört, sinnvoll erscheinen. Man muß den Mut des Kaufmanns bewundern, der, bedrängt von den großen Warenhausketten auf der einen Seite und in seinen Möglichkeiten eingeschränkt durch die Verlagerung des Einkaufsgeschehens auf der anderen Seite, noch das Experiment wagt, die Gestaltung seines Ladens einem progressiven Designer anzuvertrauen. Überhaupt scheint der Kaufmann zu den wenigen zu gehören, die heute noch die Chance sehen, welche in einem außergewöhnlichen Entwurf liegt – in diesem Fall in einem unverwechselbaren Laden.

Wird die City durch eine weitgehende Entvölkerung immer mehr zu einem großen Museum, werden auch Läden mit hohen Qualitätsansprüchen mehr und mehr an die Peripherie der Stadt ziehen. Einige der großen Einkaufsstraßen des 19. Jahrhunderts (Merceria in Venedig oder Kärntner Straße in Wien) wurden bereits dem Massentourismus überlassen; an die Stelle der Qualität trat hier die Quantität, an die Stelle berühmter Läden billige Souvenirgeschäfte voll von Waren, die nur den primitivsten Geschmack ansprechen. Läden dieser Art vertragen sich kaum mit anspruchsvollen Bauformen, mit der Einmaligkeit gewagter Architekturvisionen. In den Randbereichen der Stadt, in die sich das Leben immer mehr verlagert, ist nicht so sehr der gute Laden gefragt, sondern das Großkaufhaus, der Billigladen, das von Hunderten von Autos umgebene Einkaufszentrum. Die Chance für den gut gestalteten Laden besteht hier nur noch innerhalb des meist einheitlich gestalteten Großraums eines dieser Zentren.

Zu einem echten Problem für die Entwicklung einer neuen Architektursprache im Ladenbau wird der sich immer stärker auswirkende Denkmalschutz. So positiv sich der Schutz ganzer Bereiche auswirken mag, so gefährlich können überspitzte Forderungen für das Baugeschehen einer Stadt werden. Bereichsschutz für eine ganze City, wie er für viele Städte, etwa für die Wiener Innenstadt, bereits besteht, bewirkt letztlich das Abwandern belebender Organismen – vorerst der Bewohner selbst, dann auch von Organisationen und Büros und schließlich des Kaufmanns, ob es nun die anonyme Kaufhauskette ist oder der selbständige Kleinunternehmer. Die Tragik einer rein historisierenden Auffassung der Stadtentwicklung besteht im vorhersehbaren Tod der City, in der Verwandlung ganzer Stadtteile in riesige Museen, die eines Tages von der Allgemeinheit nicht mehr erhalten werden können. Massentourismus ist kein Ersatz für pulsierendes Leben – das hat uns letztlich das Schicksal Venedigs gezeigt.

Die Schwierigkeit besteht indessen auch für den einzelnen Laden selbst. Ein Einordnen in eine gut gestaltete Fassade vergangener Jahrhunderte ist durchaus denkbar – wie aber kann einem Architekten unserer Zeit zugemutet werden, etwa ein Rokokoportal nachzubauen, wobei die Probleme der Fertigung oder vielmehr des Nachbauens nicht allein finanzieller Natur sind.

Die Praxis des Ladenbaus ist die einer jeden anderen Bauaufgabe, sieht man einmal vom Umfang der notwendigen Arbeiten ab. Sie verlangt vom Planenden in besonderem Maß

The requirements, which are more or less the same in all branches, are very soon established during negotiations with the client. Only where exhibition rooms or facilities for "arranging" activities, e.g. travel agencies, are concerned, do the basic requirements vary.

The shop-owner generally has very definite ideas on the organization and spatial layout of his shop, to which the architect will add his own considerations. One of the architect's main difficulties is to render his formal concepts compatible with the very exacting requirements of sales practice. A detailed theoretical discussion on this aspect is almost impossible, since the individual prerequisites – location, company image, quality of the fundamental ideas, attitude of the client to the formal problems – are too varied.

A large number of contrasting aspects must be taken into consideration: let us examine the problem of the shop-window, the façade. Here, the open-front solution can be just as effective as mysterious seclusion. It must be possible to see into a display room from outside – a jewellery shop can attract its customers with small show-cases, and sales transactions here (which usually involve large sums of money) can be concluded in closed, intimate areas. A closed shop front which nevertheless affords a view into the interior can be as equally effective for advertising purposes as the long window passage where most of the articles sold in the shop can be seen by pedestrians.

While attempting to find the correct solution for such questions of detail, it is important to bear in mind that the predominant task of the architect is to create a spatial setting for the sale of goods, which immediately evokes in the customer a feeling of well-being that encourages him to linger. This is and always has been the fundamental principle of good shop design.

25. First of August fashion shop, New York.
George Ranalli.

25. Modegeschäft First of August, New York.
George Ranalli.

26. Pocket book department of the Morawa & Co.
bookshop, Vienna. Karl and Eva Mang.

26. Taschenbuchabteilung der Buchhandlung
Morawa & Co., Wien. Karl und Eva Mang.

27. Lanvin boutique, Zurich. Robert Haussmann
and Trix Haussmann-Högl.
28. Pfeifenarchiv, Stuttgart. Arbeitsgemeinschaft für Architektur und Produktgestaltung
(Peter Haas, Günter Hermann and Werner
Schwarz).
29. Schullin jewellery shop, Vienna.
Hans Hollein.

27. Boutique Lanvin, Zürich. Robert Haussmann
und Trix Haussmann-Högl.
28. Pfeifenarchiv, Stuttgart. Arbeitsgemeinschaft für Architektur und Produktgestaltung
(Peter Haas, Günter Hermann und Werner
Schwarz).
29. Juweliergeschäft Schullin, Wien.
Hans Hollein.

Präzision im Ablauf der Bautätigkeit, vor allem in der Koordination der ausführenden Firmen, die ja nur zu oft auf kleinstem Raum zu arbeiten haben. Die Termine der Eröffnung sind zumeist schon beim Entwurfsbeginn fixiert – sie sind abhängig etwa vom Beginn der Verkaufssaison, von Urlaubszeiten usw. Die Zeitspanne für den tatsächlichen Umbau ist äußerst knapp bemessen, setzt also genaueste Planung voraus.

Diese Planung hat vorerst die rein technischen Aspekte des Verkaufs zu beachten. Beim Gespräch mit dem Bauherrn zeigen sich sehr rasch die Erfordernisse, die in allen Branchen mehr oder weniger ähnlich sind. Lediglich dort, wo es sich um Ausstellungsräume oder um Einrichtungen für »Vermittlung« von Tätigkeiten, etwa um Reisebüros, handelt, werden die Grunderfordernisse etwas anders sein.

Normalerweise wird der Geschäftsinhaber sehr konkrete Vorstellungen über die Organisation und die räumliche Gliederung seines Ladens haben, an die der Architekt seine Überlegungen anschließen kann. Eine der Hauptschwierigkeiten wird für diesen darin bestehen, seine formale Idee mit den harten Erfordernissen der Verkaufspraxis in Einklang zu bringen. Im einzelnen darüber theoretisch zu diskutieren, ist fast unmöglich, da die jeweiligen Voraussetzungen – Standort, Firmenimage, Qualität der grundsätzlichen Ideen, Einstellung des Bauherrn zu formalen Problemen – zu verschieden sind.

Viele gegensätzliche Gesichtspunkte sind zu erwägen: Sehen wir uns lediglich das Problem des Schaufensters, der Straßenfront an. Hier kann die völlige Öffnung ebenso zum Erfolg führen wie das geheimnisvolle Verschließen. Ein Ausstellungsraum braucht die Einsicht von außen, ein Juwelierladen kann mit kleinen Vitrinen locken und das Verkaufsgespräch (bei dem es zumeist um große Geldbeträge geht) in intime und abgeschlossene Bereiche legen. Eine geschlossene, jedoch einsehbare Ladenfront kann ebenso als Werbemittel wirken wie die tiefe Passage, die schon dem Fußgänger die meisten der im Geschäft geführten Waren anzeigt.

Über der Suche nach der richtigen Antwort auf solche Detailfragen darf jedoch nie die Tatsache aus dem Blickfeld geraten, daß es eine entscheidende Aufgabe des Architekten ist, für die Ware einen Raum zu schaffen, der beim Käufer schon von vornherein ein Wohlbefinden auslöst, der sozusagen zum Verweilen auffordert. Dies war und ist das Grundprinzip des gut gestalteten Ladens.

1

Wollenhof textile shop, Berne
Architects: Arbeitsgruppe für rationelles Bauen (Urs Hettich)
Interior designer: Verena Huber; assistants: Ursula Feller and Gabriella Bettina

The objective of the conversion of the long-established Wollenhof textile shop in the centre of the old part of Berne was not only to display the variety of goods to greater advantage, but also to improve existing working conditions.
The departments for wool, socks, stockings and ties are accomodated on the ground floor, and are accessible from the narrow side under the arcades. They are distinguishable by an unobstrusive colouring. The salesroom is accentuated by the rear wall where the profuse display of knitting wool has been arranged in a continuous colour sequence between dark-coloured vertical elements.
The design of the children's department has flexible fittings based on a grid dimension of 51 cm. It allows for possible alterations and relates, through play areas, to a child's world of fantasy.

Textilfachgeschäft Wollenhof, Bern
Architekten: Arbeitsgruppe für rationelles Bauen (Urs Hettich)
Innenarchitektin: Verena Huber; Mitarbeiterinnen: Ursula Feller und Gabriella Bettina

In dem alteingesessenen Fachgeschäft Wollenhof, zentral in der Altstadt von Bern gelegen, sollte durch den Umbau nicht nur das Sortiment wirkungsvoller zur Geltung gebracht werden; es ging auch darum, die Arbeitsbedingungen zu verbessern.
Im Erdgeschoß, von der Schmalseite im Schutz der gedeckten Berner Lauben zugänglich, befinden sich die Abteilungen Wolle, Socken, Strümpfe und Krawatten, markiert durch eine zurückhaltende Farbgebung. Einen besonderen Akzent erhielt der Verkaufsraum durch die Rückwand, in der, durch dunkle Vertikalelemente gegliedert, das reichhaltige Angebot an Strickwolle in einem kontinuierlichen Farbablauf angeordnet wurde.
Die Gestaltung der Kinderabteilung im Obergeschoß nimmt durch die flexible Einrichtung im Rastermaß von 51 cm Rücksicht auf mögliche Veränderungen und bezieht sich mit Einbauten von Spielbereichen auf die Vorstellungswelt des Kinds.

1. The salesroom on the ground floor. On the rear wall the profuse display of knitting wool has been arranged in a continuous colour sequence between wooden vertical elements.
2. On the other walls we find elements of aluminium sheets, which, in their form, are adapted to widely differing functions.
3. Sheet-metal elements for periodicals.
4. Sheet-metal elements for wool.
5. Sheet-metal elements for hanging files with knitting patterns.
6. Part of the rear wall divided by wooden elements.

1. Der Verkaufsraum im Erdgeschoß. In der durch hölzerne Vertikalelemente gegliederten Rückwand wurde das reichhaltige Angebot an Strickwolle in einem kontinuierlichen Farbablauf angeordnet.
2. An den übrigen Wänden finden sich Elemente aus Aluminiumblech, die in ihrer Ausbildung den verschiedenartigsten Funktionen angepaßt sind.
3. Blechelemente für Zeitschriften.
4. Blechelemente für Wolle.
5. Blechelemente für Hängeregistratur mit Strickanleitungen.
6. Ausschnitt aus der durch Holzelemente gegliederten Rückwand.

3

5

2

4

6

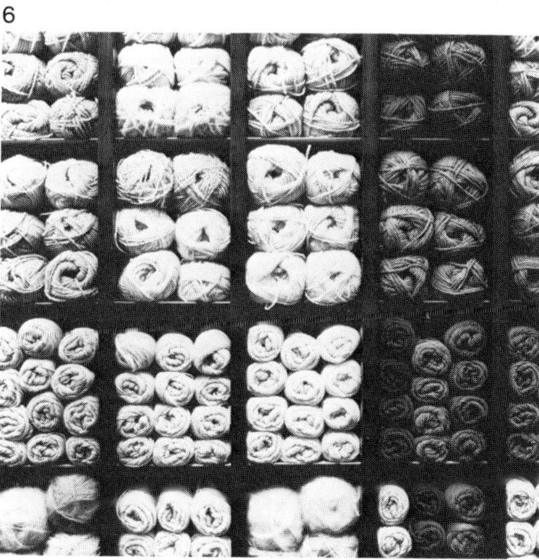

7–9. The children's department on the upper floor.

7–9. Die Kinderabteilung im Obergeschoß.

7

8

9

1. Entrance front. Renovation has restored the classicistic character of the façade as far as possible.

1. Eingangsfront. Bei der Renovierung wurde der klassizistische Charakter der Fassade so weit wie möglich wieder hergestellt.

1

Hand'art handicraft shop, Zurich
Architect: Verena Huber

The original concept behind the Hand'art handicraft shop, situated on the Neumarkt in the old part of Zurich, was to create a centre which, in addition to supplying the basic materials for the diverse techniques of textile handicraft, would also encourage the stimulating exchange of new ideas. To promote the "Do-it-yourself" idea, customers are given the opportunity to seek the advice of experts who are available on certain days; apart from the materials, designs in the form of brochures and paper patterns can also be obtained. Through this concept, the shop assumed more of a workshop character and accordingly the fittings and materials used for the interior are of the simplest nature.
The classicistic character of the shop front was not affected by the renovation; on the contrary, through the removal of a showcase it was restored to its original form.

Handarbeitsladen Hand'art, Zürich
Architektin: Verena Huber

Der Laden Hand'art am Neumarkt in der Züricher Altstadt wurde nicht nur als reines Verkaufsgeschäft konzipiert; neben seiner Aufgabe, dem Verkauf von Grundmaterialien für die verschiedensten textilen Verarbeitungstechniken zu dienen, sollte er auch ein Umschlagplatz für Ideen werden. Zur Belebung des »Do-it-yourself«-Gedankens etwa können sich Kunden an bestimmten Tagen von Fachleuten beraten lassen; zusätzlich zu den Materialien werden auch Entwürfe in Form von Anleitungen und Schnittmustern angeboten. Durch diese Konzeption erhielt der Laden mehr den Charakter einer Werkstatt und bedurfte für den Innenausbau lediglich einfachster Ausstattung und Materialien.
Die Renovierung beeinträchtigte den klassizistischen Charakter der Ladenfront nicht; durch die Entfernung eines Schaukastens sorgte man im Gegenteil für die Wiederherstellung des ursprünglichen Zustands.

2. View through the right shop-window into the shop interior at night.
3–5. As the shop is meant to have more of a workshop character, the materials and details used for the interior are of the simplest nature.

2. Blick bei Nacht durch das rechte Schaufenster in das Ladeninnere.
3–5. Da der Laden mehr den Charakter einer Werkstatt erhalten sollte, beschränkte man sich beim Innenausbau auf einfachste Materialien und Details.

2

3

1

2

Valentino AG jeans shop, Spreitenbach shopping center, near Zurich
Architect: Gerd Burla

An article of clothing unparalleled in its popularity, jeans have become a symbol of our era and an embodiment of youth and vitality. With this in mind the overall concept of the Valentino AG jeans shop, which is located in the Spreitenbach shopping centre, near Zurich, presents a solution that is as simple as it is variable. A two-layer presentation stand displays the large veriety of wares to advantage and is space-saving in its function. Access to the elements in the fixed rear layer is gained by sliding the elements in the movable front layer.
The entire front view within the shopping complex also follows this principle. Some of the sheets of glass mounted on tubular steel supports are movable and arranged in such a way that the access opening onto the shopping parade can be varied.

Jeans-Shop Valentino AG, Einkaufszentrum Spreitenbach bei Zürich
Architekt: Gerd Burla

Wie kaum ein anderes Bekleidungsstück sind die Jeans ein Symbol unserer Zeit, Ausdruck für Jugend und Beweglichkeit. Die darauf abgestimmte Gesamtkonzeption des im Einkaufszentrum Spreitenbach bei Zürich gelegenen Jeans-Shop Valentino AG ist ebenso einfach wie variabel. Die Wahl eines zweischichtigen Präsentiergestells erlaubte es, das mannigfaltige Angebot platzsparend und übersichtlich darzubieten. Durch Verschieben der Einheiten in der vorderen, mobilen Schicht werden alle Einheiten in der festen, rückwärtigen Schicht zugänglich.
Auch die Frontlösung innerhalb des Großraums des Shopping-Centers entspricht diesem Prinzip: Die Glasplatten, von Stahlrohrbügeln getragen, sind teilweise mobil und so angeordnet, daß verschiedene Varianten der Öffnung zur Ladenstraße möglich werden.

1. Movable front element.
2. View through one of the front elements towards the presentation stand on the back wall of the salesroom.
3. The presentation stand consists of a movable front layer and a fixed rear layer.
4. The changing cubicles are also movable and can be positioned as required.
5. Axonometric view. Key: 1 movable front element, 2 fixed front element, 3 sales boxes, 4 changing cubicle, 5 movable layer of the presentation stand.

1. Mobiles Frontelement.
2. Blick durch eines der Frontelemente auf das Präsentiergestell an der Rückwand des Verkaufsraumes.
3. Das Präsentiergestell besteht aus einer mobilen vorderen und einer festen rückwärtigen Schicht.
4. Auch die Anprobekabinen sind mobil und können daher an beliebiger Stelle aufgestellt werden.
5. Axonometrie. Legende: 1 mobiles Frontelement, 2 festes Frontelement, 3 Verkaufskorpus, 4 Anprobekabinen, 5 mobile Schicht des Präsentiergestells.

3

4

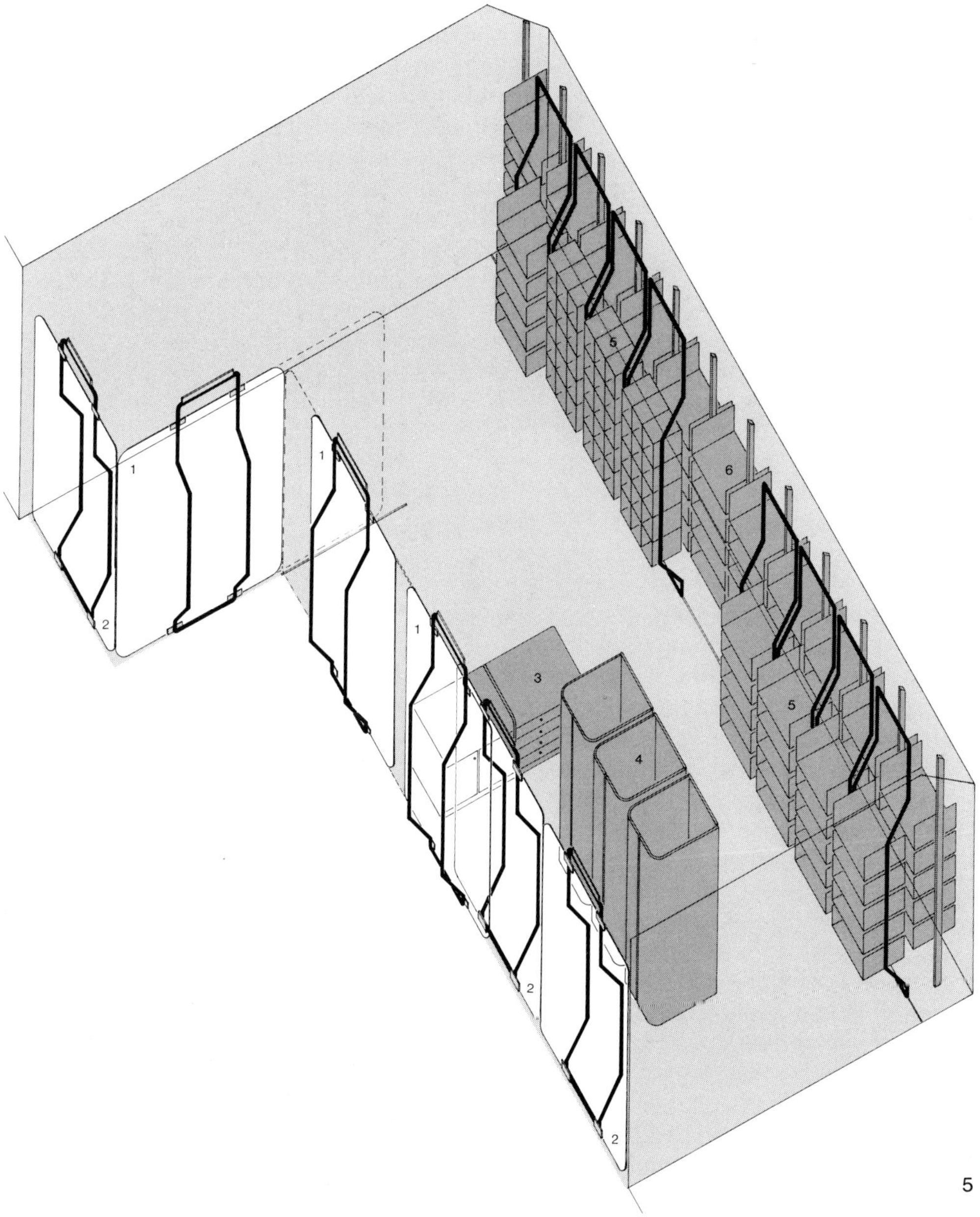

5

6

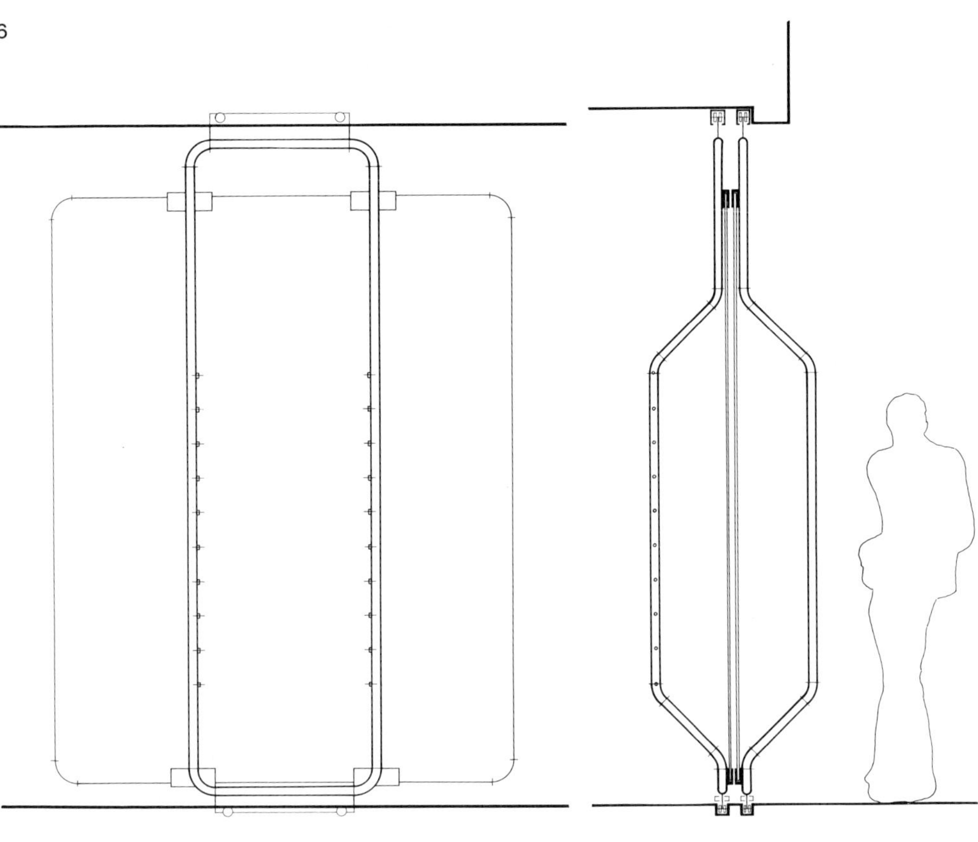

6. Detail of a movable front element (on the left elevation, on the right section).
7. Detail of the presentation stand (on the left elevation of a movable element, on the right section through the fixed and the movable layer).
8. View onto the movable front layer of the presentation stand.

6. Detail eines mobilen Fassadenelements (links Ansicht, rechts Schnitt).
7. Detail des Präsentiergestells (links Ansicht eines beweglichen Elements, rechts Schnitt durch die feste und die mobile Schicht).
8. Blick auf die mobile vordere Schicht des Präsentiergestells.

7

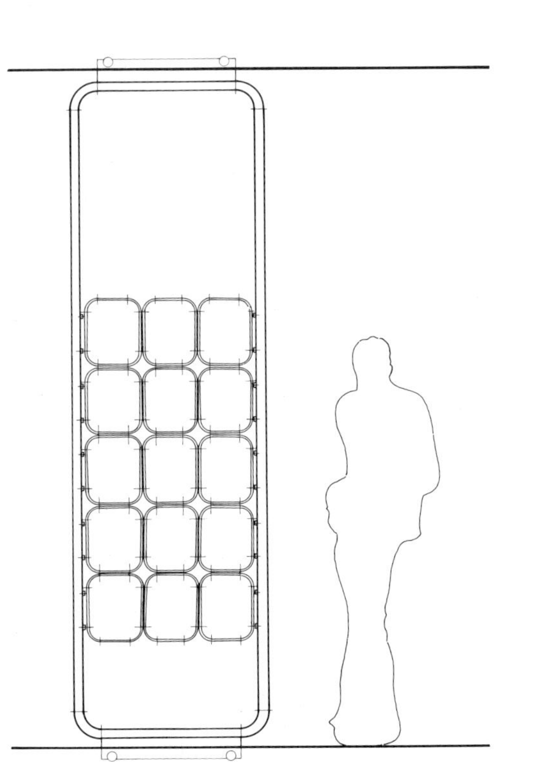

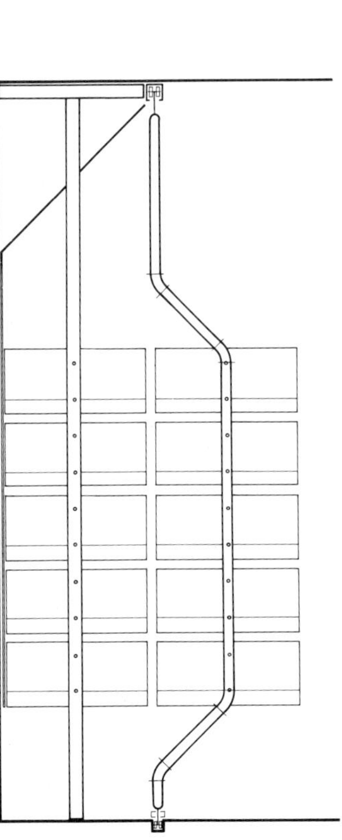

Carnaby boutique, La Coruña, Spain
Architects: Interplay (Diethelm Lenze)

In designing the Carnaby boutique, the architect has completely broken away from the principles of conventional shop architecture. The interplay of colours and forms, lively and full of wit, invalidates the general rules of design. This can already be seen at the façade of the building, the whole of which has been converted into the billboard for an unconventional advertisement. The interior, a cave-like structure in gypsum, provides an effective setting for the displayed goods, which hang on movable tubular steel frames.

Boutique Carnaby, La Coruña, Spanien
Architekten: Interplay (Diethelm Lenze)

Bei der Gestaltung der Boutique Carnaby wurde von den Prinzipien herkömmlicher Ladenbauarchitektur völlig abgegangen. Ein Spiel von Farben und Formen, leicht beschwingt und voll Witz, setzt alle üblichen Regeln außer Kraft. Das beginnt bereits bei der Fassade des Hauses, die in ihrer Gesamtheit zum Träger einer unkonventionellen Werbung umfunktioniert wurde. Der Innenraum ist ein höhlenartiges Gebilde aus Gips, das mit seinen bewegten Formen einen effektvollen Hintergrund für die ausgestellten Waren bildet, die auf fahrbaren Stahlrohrgestellen hängen.

1. The façade of the building, the whole of which has been converted into the billboard for an unconventional advertisment.
2–4. The interior, a cave-like structure in gypsum, provides an effective setting for the goods displayed.

1. Die Fassade des Hauses wurde in ihrer Gesamtheit zum Träger einer unkonventionellen Werbung umfunktioniert.
2–4. Der Innenraum ist ein höhlenartiges Gebilde aus Gips, das mit seinen bewegten Formen einen effektvollen Hintergrund für die ausgestellten Waren bildet.

1, 2. Walls and ceilings bathe in the festive light of 80 ball lamps. The fixtures, which are combined in a grid system, are movable (mounted on wheels).
3, 4. The boutique is accommodated in a basement room below an arcade in the old part of Berne.
5. Plan, longitudinal and cross section.

1, 2. Die Wände und Decken lassen sich mit 80 Kugelleuchten in festliches Licht tauchen. Die Rastermöbel sind fahrbar (auf Rädern montiert).
3, 4. Die Boutique wurde in einem Kellerraum unter einem Laubengang in der Berner Altstadt eingerichtet.
5. Grundriß, Längsschnitt und Querschnitt.

1

Box boutique, Berne
Architect: Ubald Klug

The Box boutique is accommodated in a basement room below an arcade in the old part of Berne. Red arrows imprinted in the asphalt and signs in the covered gallery point in the direction of the stairway to the boutique rooms.
The angular, mirrored walls of the stairway allow the shop's interior to be seen from the street. The inside of the boutique resembles a tunnel. Walls and ceilings are lined with highly polished metal panels and bathed in the festive light of 80 ball lamps of opalescent glass. The display fixtures, which are combined in a grid system, are movable (mounted on wheels) and consist of white painted wood.

Boutique Box, Bern
Architekt: Ubald Klug

Die Boutique Box wurde in einem Kellerraum unter einem Laubengang in der Berner Altstadt eingerichtet. Im Asphalt eingedrückte rote Pfeile und Zeichen im gedeckten Laubengang weisen auf den Abgang zu den Räumen der Boutique.
Die übereck verspiegelten Wände ermöglichen schon von der Straße her einen Einblick in das Geschäftsinnere. Der Innenraum gleicht einem Tunnel. Die Wände und Decken wurden mit stark glänzenden Platten verkleidet und lassen sich mit 80 Kugelleuchten aus Milchglas in festliches Licht tauchen. Die Rastermöbel zum Hängen der Ware sind fahrbar (auf Rädern montiert) und bestehen aus weiß lackiertem Holz.

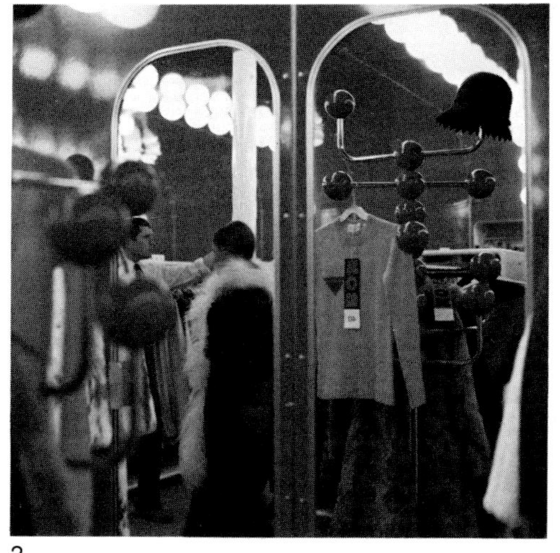

2

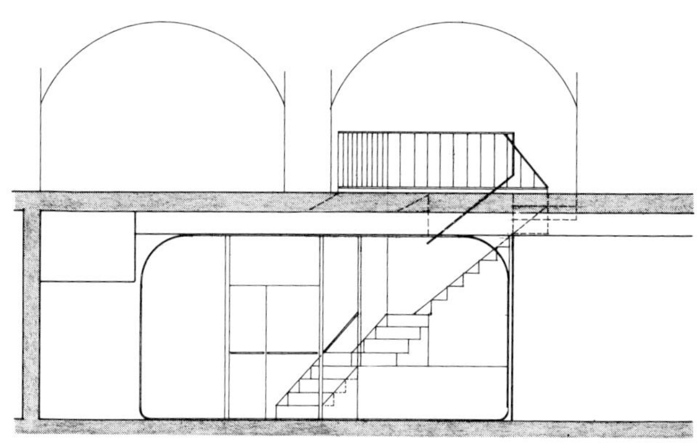

5

3

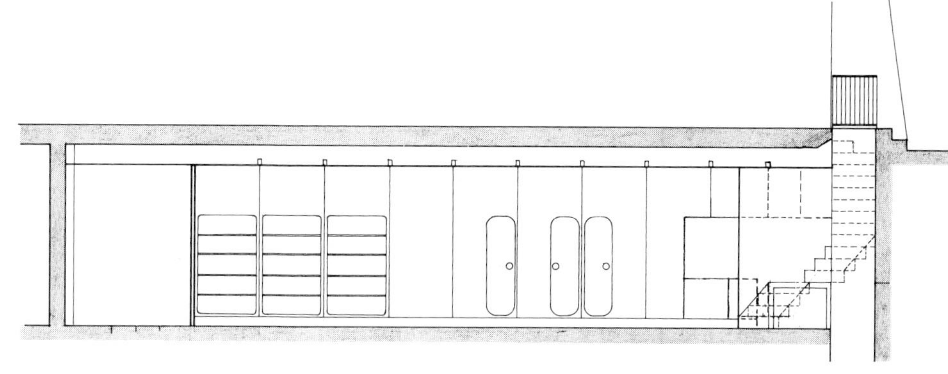

4

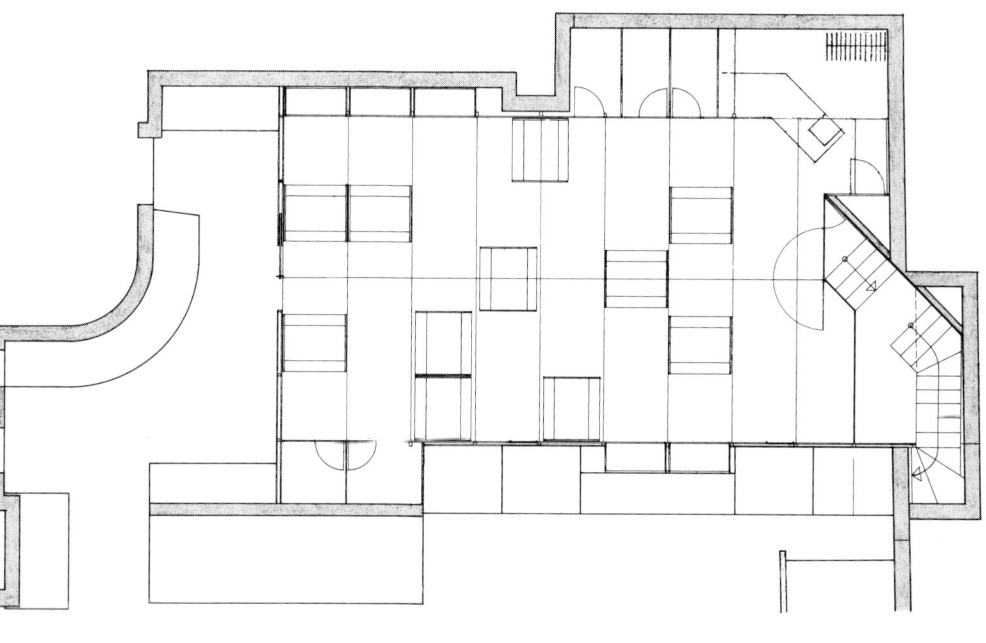

1

2

Quantas boutique, Vigo, Spain
Architects: Interplay (Natalio Arnoso and Diethelm Lenze)

The atmosphere in the Quantas boutique is uncomplicated and non-professional. The unusual from of the entrance, which appears to be a mere hole in the brick wall separating the shop from the street, incites the curiosity of passers-by who are then prompted to take a closer look inside. The staircase, a very dominating element, is located directly opposite the cash desk near the entrance, so that customers have immediate access to the basement area – a visual separation which is simultaneously a spatial link.
The interior arrangement is very simple: boxes function as display stands, articles of clothing hang on washing-lines. Everything is "fluid" and designed with humour – it is a shop full of surprises.

Boutique Quantas, Vigo, Spanien
Architekten: Interplay (Natalio Arnoso und Diethelm Lenze)

In der Boutique Quantas herrscht eine völlig unkomplizierte, unprofessionelle Stimmung. Eine Ziegelwand mit einem wie ausgebrochen wirkenden Eingang trennt zwar den Laden von der Straße, lädt aber gleichzeitig durch ihre ungewöhnliche Form zum Nähertreten ein. Die beherrschende Treppe wurde direkt gegenüber dem Kassenbereich nahe dem Eingang angeordnet, so daß der Besucher sofort den Weg in das Untergeschoß findet – eine optische Trennung und räumliche Verbindung zugleich.
Die Innenräume sind sehr einfach gehalten: Kisten bilden Stellagen, die Kleidungsstücke hängen zum Teil an Wäscheleinen. Alles ist »im Fluß« und mit Humor gestaltet – ein Laden voll von überraschenden Effekten.

1. The interior arrangement is very simple.
Everything is "fluid" and designed with humour.
2. The unusual form of the entrance, which
appears to be a mere hole in the brick wall,
incites the curiosity of passers-by.
3. Plan (ground floor) and section. Key:
1 entrance, 2 cash desk, 3 downstairs, 4 upstairs,
5 phone booth, 6 changing cubicle.
4. Basement.
5. Ground floor.
6. The stairs going upwards.

1. Die Innenräume sind sehr einfach gehalten.
Alles ist im »Fluß« und mit Humor gestaltet.
2. Eine Ziegelwand mit einem wie ausgebrochen
wirkenden Eingang lädt durch ihre ungewöhnliche Form zum Nähertreten ein.
3. Grundriß (Erdgeschoß) und Schnitt. Legende:
1 Eingang, 2 Kasse, 3 Treppe nach unten,
4 Treppe nach oben, 5 Telephonkabine, 6 Anklei-
dekabine.
4. Untergeschoß.
5. Erdgeschoß.
6. Die Treppe nach oben.

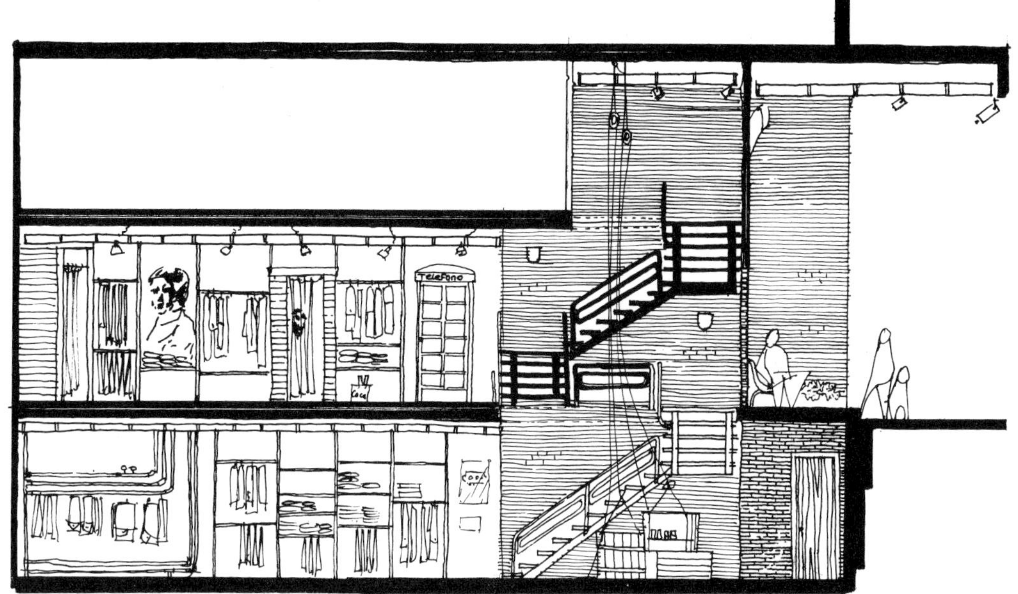

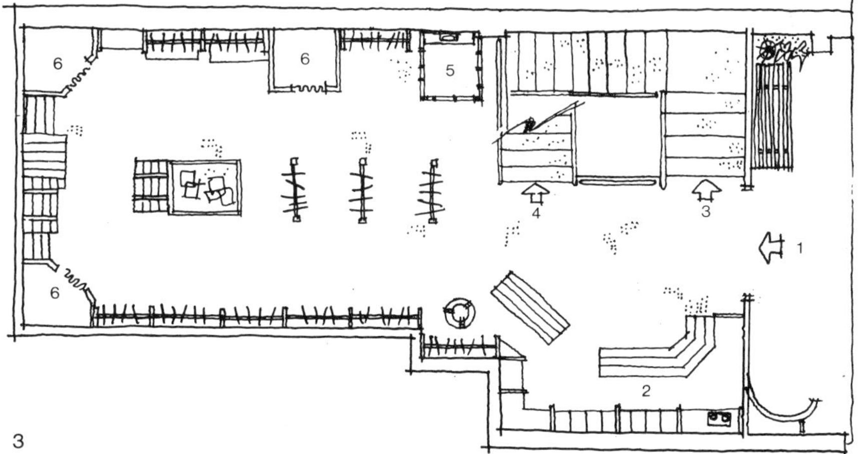

3

4

5

6

1. Plan. Key: 1 entrance, 2 display, 3 suspended tube, 4 changing cubicle, 5 sales, 6 store.
2. Entrance front.

1. Grundriß. Legende: 1 Eingang, 2 Ausstellung, 3 hängende Röhre, 4 Anprobekabine, 5 Verkauf, 6 Lager.
2. Eingangsfront.

2

André Courrèges boutique, Boston
Architects: Stull Associates

In the design of the Courrèges boutique in the Chestnut Hill Mall on the outskirts of Boston, an attempt was made to reflect the geometric style characteristic of Courrèges fashion in the interior decoration.
All lighting fixtures and the air-conditioning ducts are mounted in a suspended tube, the front end of which slightly projects over the entrance face and bears the indirectly illuminated initials – "AC" – of the fashion designer. The interior of the boutique is also a long tube, with open and closed display bays, the changing cubicles and benches cut into it. The display stands around the shop-window, the benches and the open display bays are illuminated from below to maintain the impression of structural coherency.
With the exception of the mirrored surfaces and those consisting of stainless steel, all interior surfaces are white – the plaster, wood, leather upholstery and woolen carpet. The mirrors and the ingenious lighting arrangement make the room appear much larger than it really is.

André Courrèges Boutique, Boston
Architekten: Stull Associates

Bei der Gestaltung der Boutique von Courrèges, an der Chestnut Hill Mall im Randbereich von Boston gelegen, wurde versucht, den geometrischen Stil der Mode von Courrèges in das Vokabular der Innenraumgestaltung zu übertragen.
Eine hängende Röhre enthält sämtliche Beleuchtungskörper und die Klimakanäle und ist an der Stirnseite, die ein kleines Stück über die Eingangsfront hinausragt, mit den indirekt beleuchteten Anfangsbuchstaben des Modeschöpfers – »AC« – versehen. Auch der Innenraum selbst ist eine lange Röhre, in die teils offene, teils geschlossene Ausstellungsnischen, die Anprobekabinen sowie Sitzbänke eingeschnitten sind. Die Auslagentische im Schaufensterbereich, die Sitzbänke und die offenen Ausstellungsnischen sind von unten beleuchtet, um den Eindruck einer zusammenhängenden Struktur soweit wie möglich zu erhalten.
Alle Oberflächen in der Boutique, die nicht verspiegelt sind oder aus rostfreiem Stahl bestehen, sind weiß – der Putz, das Holz, die Lederpolsterung und der Wollteppich. Durch die Spiegel und eine geschickte Beleuchtung wirkt der Raum wesentlich größer, als er tatsächlich ist.

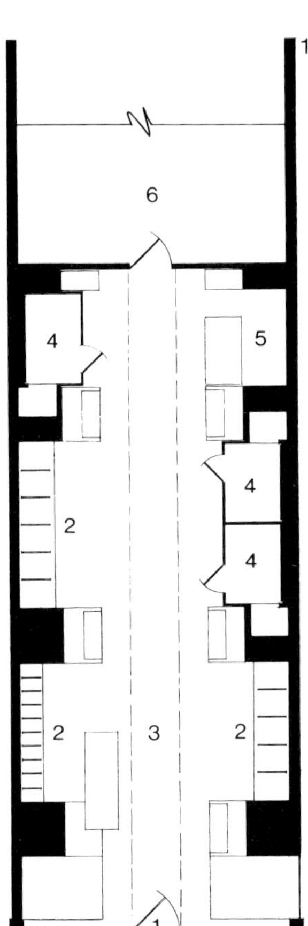

The salesroom, picture 3.

3–5. The salesroom is a long tube, with open and closed display bays, the changing cubicles and benches cut into it. Another tube suspended from above contains all lighting fixtures and the air-conditioning ducts.

3–5. Der Verkaufsraum ist eine lange Röhre, in die teils offene, teils geschlossene Ausstellungsnischen, die Anprobekabinen sowie Sitzbänke eingeschnitten sind. Eine darin eingehängte weitere Röhre enthält sämtliche Beleuchtungskörper und die Klimakanäle.

Very Very Terry Jerry fashion shop, San Francisco
Architects: Esherick, Homsey, Dodge and Davis

The Very Very Terry Jerry ladies' fashion shop was located in the Cannery, a well-known shopping and amusement centre around Fisherman's Wharf which came into being in 1968 in the course of the reconstruction of a brick building erected shortly after the turn of the century. In operation for just two years, the shop contained a wide range of articles which catered mainly to young people.
The concept of the shop was based on the idea that shopping can be a spectacle, an adventure – that women would find it fun to playact while trying on clothes. The interior layout of the shop was designed to promote the spatial dramatization of this procedure. The rooms, located on different levels, opened onto one another, forming a circular passageway from one end of the shop to the other.

Modegeschäft Very Very Terry Jerry, San Francisco
Architekten: Esherick, Homsey, Dodge and Davis

Das Damenmodegeschäft Very Very Terry Jerry, das eine breite Verkaufspalette für die Jugend bot (es existierte nur zwei Jahre), befand sich in dem weithin bekannt gewordenen Einkaufs- und Unterhaltungskomplex The Cannery im Gebiet Fisherman's Wharf, der 1968 durch den Umbau eines kurz nach der Jahrhundertwende errichteten Backsteingebäudes entstand.
Das Konzept des Ladens beruhte auf der Idee, daß Einkauf ein Schauspiel, ein Abenteuer sein kann, daß Frauen ein Vergnügen daran haben, Rollen zu spielen oder zu wechseln, während sie die Kleider anprobieren. Der Laden war so eingerichtet, daß dieser Vorgang räumlich dramatisiert wurde. Der Ablauf der ineinanderfließenden Räume, die man auf verschiedenen Höhen angeordnet hatte, war als Rundgang ausgebildet gewesen.

1. View onto one of the narrow sides of the shops and into the open covered walkway between sidewalk and shop.
2. Cashier area.
3. Plan and sections. Key: 1 jewellery, 2 bags, 3 cash desk and wrapping counter, 4 shoes, 5 stockings, 6 gifts, 7 cosmetics, 8 changing cubicles, 9 bridge.
4. The lightly recessed entrance area.
5. View from the cosmetics area into the changing area.

1. Blick auf eine der Schmalseiten des Geschäfts und in den offenen überdeckten Gang zwischen Gehweg und Geschäft.
2. Kassenbereich.
3. Grundriß und Schnitte. Legende: 1 Schmuck, 2 Taschen, 3 Kasse und Packplatz, 4 Schuhe, 5 Strümpfe, 6 Geschenke, 7 Kosmetika, 8 Anproberäume, 9 Brücke.
4. Die leicht eingezogene Eingangszone.
5. Blick vom Bereich für Kosmetika in den Anprobebereich.

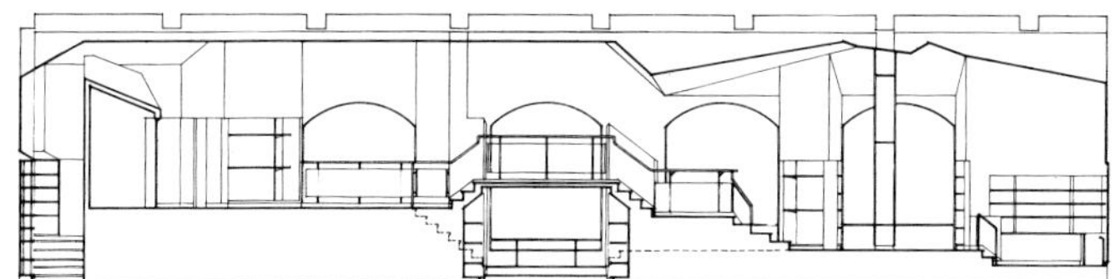
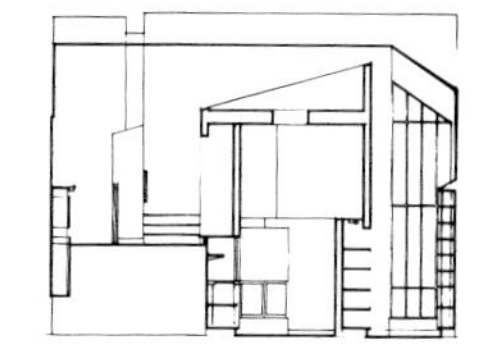
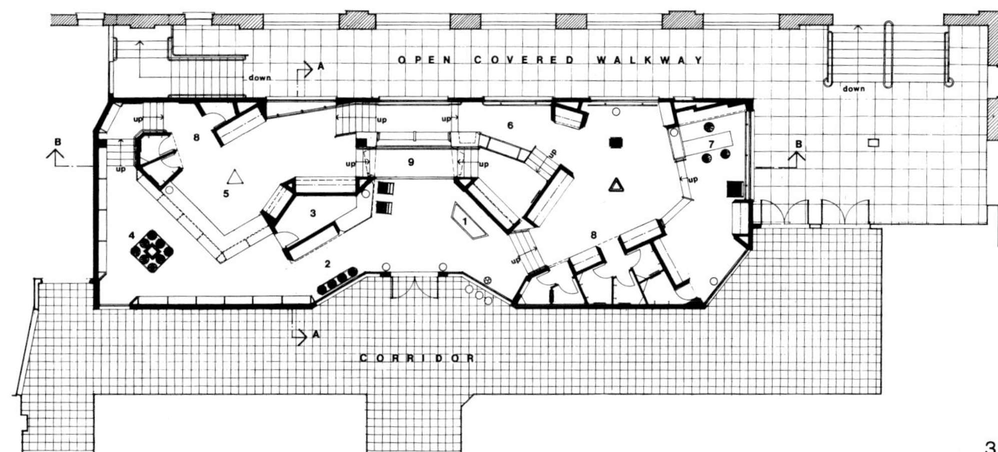

3

4

5

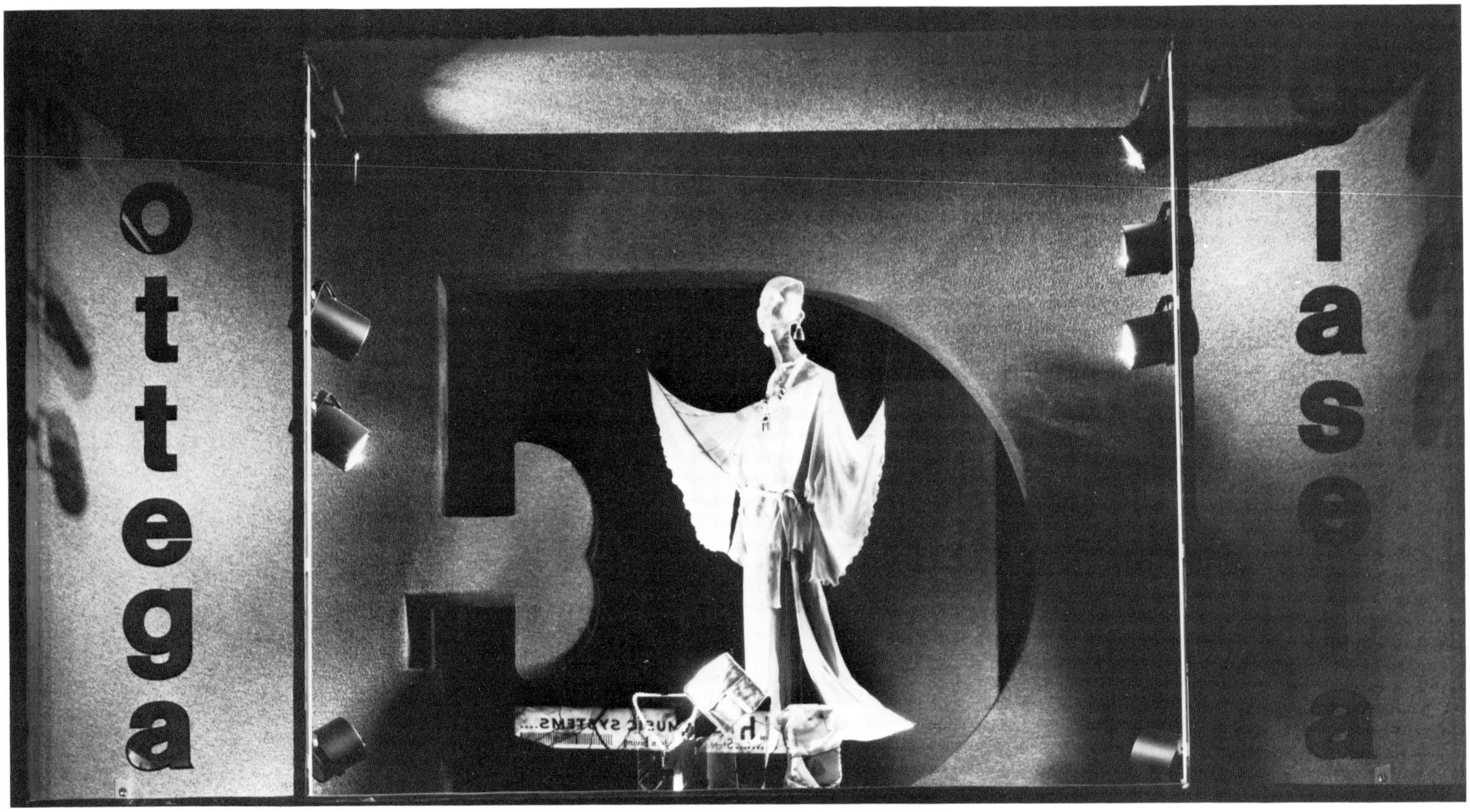

1

Bottega Glaseia fashion shop, Chicago
Architects: Stanley Tigerman and Associates

The programme for the Bottega Glaseia was to create a complete design concept, including the design of an eye-catching symbol for the firm.
Primary consideration was given to the symbol: it served as the basis for the other graphics – labels, boxes, carrier bags, invoices etc. – as well as for the design of the salesroom itself, which takes on gently sweeping forms. All surfaces – floors, walls and ceiling – are covered with dark grey carpeting, which gives visual uniformity to the flowing forms and provides a neutral background for the articles of clothing (which are arranged according to colour, not according to size).

Modegeschäft Bottega Glaseia, Chicago
Architekten: Stanley Tigerman and Associates

Das Programm für die Bottega Glaseia beinhaltete die Entwicklung eines vollständigen Gestaltungskonzepts, worin auch der Entwurf eines markanten Firmenzeichens eingeschlossen war.
Dieses Zeichen wurde zuerst in Angriff genommen und diente als Ausgangspunkt sowohl für die übrigen graphischen Lösungen – Etiketten, Schachteln, Tragetaschen, Rechnungen usw. – als auch für die Gestaltung des Verkaufsraums selbst, der sich in weichen runden Formen präsentiert. Alle Oberflächen – Boden, Wände und Decke – wurden mit einem dunkelgrauen Teppich überzogen, der die fließenden Formen auch vom Material her zusammenbindet und einen neutralen Hintergrund für die nicht nach Größen, sondern nach Farben zusammengestellten Kleidungsstücke abgibt.

2

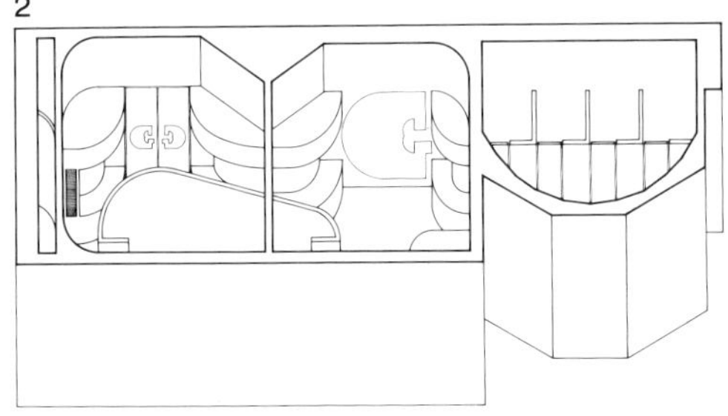

1. View from the street towards the shop-window. The symbol of the firm is the back-wall of the display, which shows only one item of clothing at a time.
2. Axonometric view, looking towards the street.
3. View from the interior onto the display.
4. Cashier area.
5. Changing area.
6. Sales area.

1. Blick von der Straße auf das Schaufenster. Das Firmenzeichen bildet die Rückwand der Auslage, in der jeweils nur ein Kleidungsstück gezeigt wird.
2. Axonometrie, gegen die Straße zu gesehen.
3. Blick vom Innenraum zur Auslage.
4. Kassenbereich.
5. Anprobebereich.
6. Verkaufsbereich.

3

4

5

6

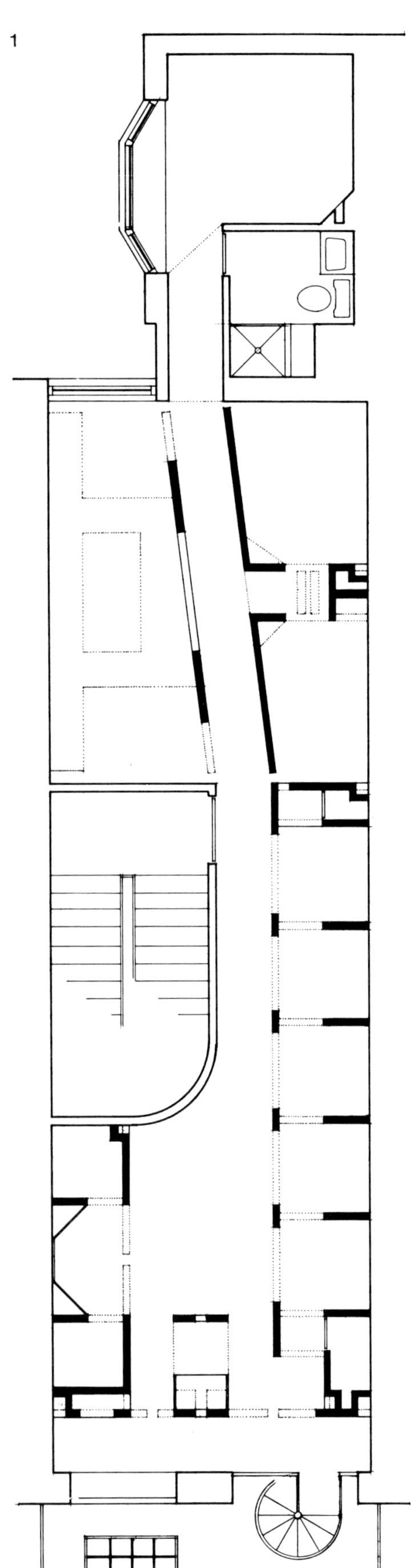

1

First of August fashion shop, New York
Architect: George Ranalli

An existing clothes' shop on the ground floor was extended to take in the floor directly above, and the range of services was increased. While retaining its original function below, with the addition of more sales space, the shop now houses a beauty salon on the upper floor.

The characteristic building feature of the area in which the shop is located are sandstone façades with projecting shop fronts. Consequently, a glass projection was erected in front of the shop, extending over both floors. The profiles of this projection, which form a grid made up of small-sized squares, blend in with the surrounding sandstone walls. Depending on the illumination, the projection may appear solid like a wall or transparent like a normal shop-window.

In accordance with its diverse functions, the upper floor is divided into two separate areas. The sales area is located at the front, with two changing cubicles on the left and five alcoves for hanging garments on the right. The rear area is reserved for the beauty salon and is separated from the front by the main staircase.

All new fittings are in white, and the old room boundaries have been painted dark blue.

Modegeschäft First of August, New York
Architekt: George Ranalli

Ein im Erdgeschoß vorhandener Laden für Bekleidung wurde durch die Einbeziehung des darüber liegenden Geschosses sowohl räumlich als auch vom Verkaufsprogramm her erweitert. Während es unten von der Funktion her beim alten blieb, findet sich jetzt im Obergeschoß neben zusätzlicher Fläche für den Verkauf von Bekleidung ein Schönheitssalon.

Für die Bebauung in dem Straßenabschnitt, in dem sich der Laden befindet, sind Sandsteinfassaden mit vorspringenden ein- oder zweigeschossigen Ladenfronten charakteristisch. In Anpassung hieran wurde vor den Laden ein über beide Geschosse gezogener Glasvorbau gesetzt, dessen Profile ein Raster aus kleinformatigen Quadraten bilden und so die Teilung der umgebenden Sandsteinwände weiterführen. Je nach Beleuchtung wirkt der Vorbau kompakt wie eine geschlossene Wand oder aber transparent wie ein normales Schaufenster.

Das neu eingerichtete Obergeschoß ist entsprechend den verschiedenen Funktionen in zwei Bereiche gegliedert. Der vordere Bereich enthält die Verkaufsfläche für Bekleidung – links zwei Anprobekabinen, rechts fünf Nischen, in denen die Kleidungsstücke aufgehängt sind. Der hintere Bereich, vom vorderen durch die Haupttreppe abgegrenzt, ist dem Schönheitssalon vorbehalten.

Alle neuen Einbauten sind weiß, während die alten Raumbegrenzungen in einem dunklen Blau gestrichen wurden.

1. Plan (upper floor).
2. A glass projection was erected in front of the shop, extending over both floors. The profiles of this projection, which form a grid made up of small-sized squares, blend in with the surrounding sandstone walls.

1. Grundriß (Obergeschoß).
2. Vor den Laden wurde ein über beide Geschosse gezogener Glasvorbau gesetzt, dessen Profile ein Raster aus kleinformatigen Quadraten bilden und so die Teilung der umgebenden Sandsteinwände weiterführen.

ughters
of Sweden Inc.
P.J. JAMRA, INC.

3

3–5. The newly opened upper floor. All new fittings are in white, while the old room boundaries have been painted dark blue.

3–5. Das neu eingerichtete Obergeschoß. Alle neuen Einbauten sind weiß, während die alten Raumbegrenzungen in einem dunklen Blau gestrichen wurden.

1. Entrance front. The upper part of the shop-window is covered with a "curtain" consisting of lightly engraved panes of glass in lead lines.

1. Eingangsfront. Der obere Teil der Schaufenster wird von einem »Vorhang« aus leicht geätzten Gläsern in Bleiverglasung bedeckt.

1

Lanvin boutique, Zurich
Architects: Robert Haussmann and Trix Haussmann-Högl

The cube-shaped salesroom, which extends over two floors, is divided into four distinct areas. Three sides are separated by alcoves. The fourth opens onto the shop front, with the entrance door positioned in its centre. Access to the upper alcoves is gained over a U-shaped gallery; this arrangement emphasises the main axis of the room. The reflections of narrow mirrored doors placed opposite one another on the front of each alcove create the illusion of an endless sequence of rooms. By using imitation materials, effects were achieved which would have been hardly possible if real materials had been used. The coating, which covers the wooden walls, the parts of the gallery and the alcoves as well as the stucco waffle ceiling, is a marble interpretation (faux-marbre technique). It is patterned like the real marble (rosso norvegia) set into the centre of the floor.

Boutique Lanvin, Zürich
Architekten: Robert Haussmann und Trix Haussmann-Högl

Der über zwei Geschosse durchlaufende, kubische Verkaufsraum wird an drei Seiten regelmäßig durch Nischen gegliedert, die vierte Seite öffnet sich gegen die Schaufensterfront mit der axial angeordneten Eingangstür. Die oberen Nischen werden über eine U-förmige Galerie erschlossen; diese Anordnung betont die Hauptachse des Raums. Die Spiegelungen in den vor jeder Nische angebrachten schmalen Spiegeltüren, die einander genau gegenüber liegen, erzeugen die Illusion einer unendlichen Folge von Räumen. Durch Materialverfremdung wurden Materialwirkungen erzielt, wie sie mit echten Materialien kaum möglich gewesen wären. Der in der Mitte des Fußbodens eingelassene echte Marmor (Rosso norvegia) diente den Malern als Vorlage für die Marmor-Interpretation (Faux-Marbre-Technik), die die aus Holz bestehenden Wände, Galerieteile und Nischen ebenso überzieht wie die aus Stuck gefertigte kassettierte Decke.

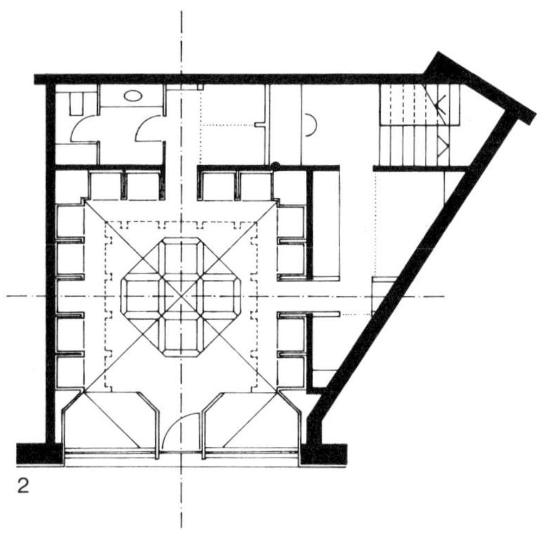

2. Plan (ground-floor level).
3. The cashier area at the rear of the salesroom.
4. The front part of the salesroom.
5. Perspective plan.
6. View from inside towards the entrance area.

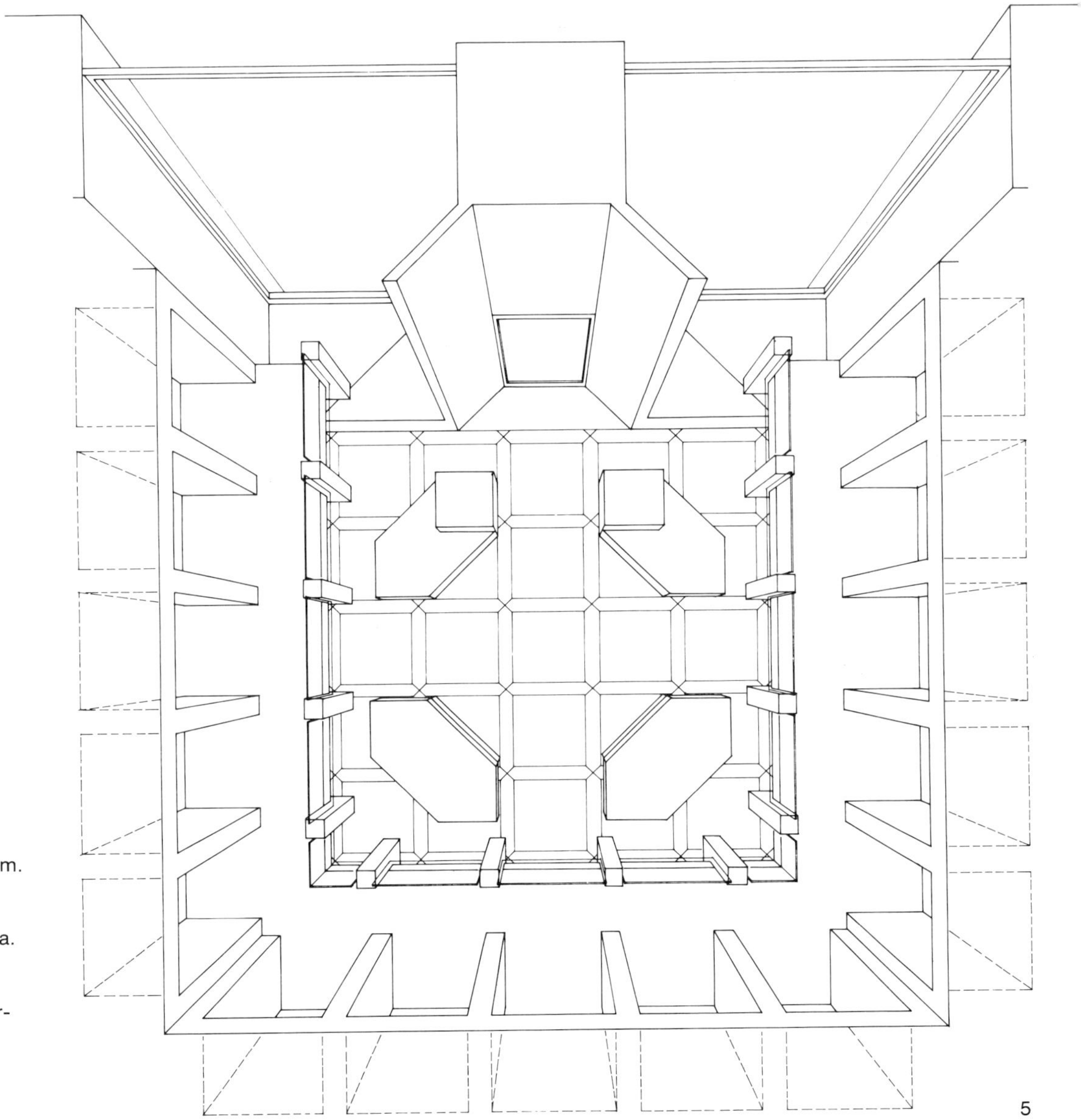

2. Grundriß (Erdgeschoßebene).
3. Der Kassenbereich im hinteren Teil des Verkaufsraumes.
4. Der vordere Teil des Verkaufsraumes.
5. Perspektivischer Grundriß.
6. Blick von innen auf den Eingangsbereich.

1

2

Levent couture-atelier, Zurich
Architect: Gerd Burla

The Levent couture-atelier was accommodated in the Baroque guildhall Zur Meisen which lies in the centre of the old part of Zurich.
Following the reconstruction of the rooms to their original form, a completely unconventional, exclusive atelier materialized which has nothing in common with the traditional conception of a haute-couture salon. The customary requisites of a fashion house – the brocade, the mirrors, the wall-to-wall carpeting – have been omitted. Instead the room itself, with its beauty, simplicity and unobtrusiveness, with its almost sacral character, creates the atmosphere that is generally associated with a house of this nature.

Couture-Atelier Levent, Zürich
Architekt: Gerd Burla

Das Couture-Atelier Levent fand seinen Platz in dem barocken Zunfthaus Zur Meisen, das zentral in der Züricher Altstadt liegt.
Nach Wiederherstellung der Räume in ihrer ursprünglichen Form entstand ein völlig unkonventionelles, exklusives Atelier, das mit der überlieferten Vorstellung eines Salons der Haute Couture nichts gemein hat. Auf alle üblichen Requisiten eines Modehauses, wie Brokat, Spiegel und Spannteppich, wurde verzichtet. Der schöne, sehr einfache und zurückhaltende, beinahe sakral wirkende Raum schafft allein aus sich heraus die Atmosphäre, die man mit einem solchen Haus verbindet.

7

3   4   5

1. View from the salesroom towards the Großmünster.
2. Salesroom. The changing cubicle is behind on
the left.
3. View from the entrance into the salesroom. On
the right behind the wall element is the atelier.
4. Salesroom. The atelier is on the left.
5. View from the entrance area over the free-
standing wall element into the atelier.
6. Plan. Key: 1 entrance, 2 salesroom, 3 atelier,
4 changing cubicle.
7. Entrance door.

1. Blick vom Verkaufsraum auf das Großmünster.
2. Verkaufsraum. Hinten links die Anprobekabine.
3. Blick vom Eingang in den Verkaufsraum.
Rechts hinter dem Wandelement das Atelier.
4. Verkaufsraum. Links das Atelier.
5. Blick vom Eingangsbereich über das frei
stehende Wandelement in das Atelier.
6. Grundriß. Legende: 1 Eingang, 2 Verkaufsraum, 3 Atelier, 4 Anprobekabine.
7. Eingangstür.

6

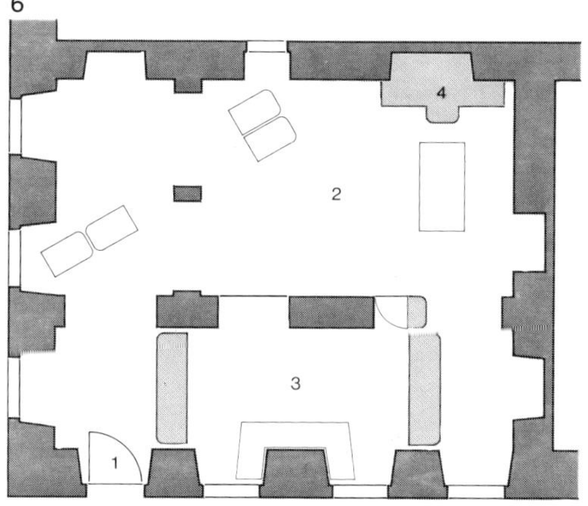

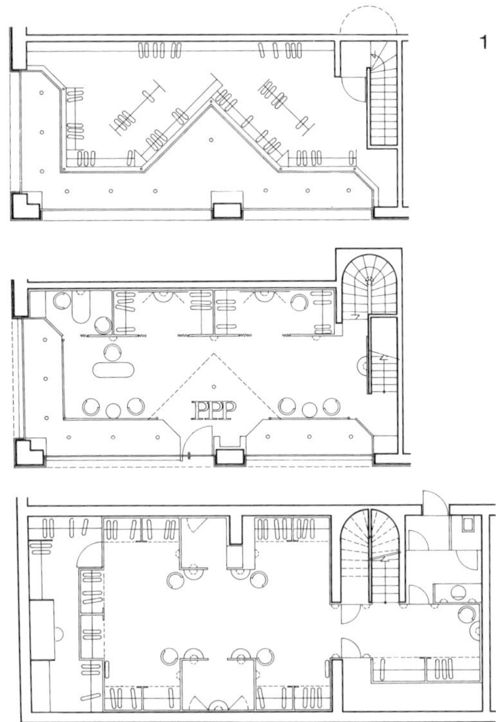

PPP fur shop, Zurich
Architects: Robert Haussmann and Trix Haussmann-Högl; assistant: Benno Weber

A limited area in the basement and a ground-floor room with a relatively high ceiling existed to be converted into the PPP (Pelz Paradies Paradeplatz) fur shop, situated at an extremely advantageous point on the Zurich Paradeplatz.
In order to obtain a spacious and elegant presentation of goods, illusionistic elements were employed. Hereby great importance was attached to the technical aspects such as lighting, air-conditioning and safety devices.
An optical enlargement of the main room on the ground-flor is mainly achieved by the mirror plates on the outer surfaces of the gallery and by the large lighting elements hanging in front of it, their shape accentuating the high ceiling.
The colour scheme, comprised of warm beige tones which harmonize equally well with the tinted and crystal-clear mirrors and with the gold tone of the bronze fittings, create an atmosphere befitting the precious furs.

Pelzgeschäft PPP, Zürich
Architekten: Robert Haussmann und Trix Haussmann-Högl; Mitarbeiter: Benno Weber

Für den Umbau des Pelzgeschäfts PPP (Pelz Paradies Paradeplatz), das sich einer hervorragenden Verkaufslage am Züricher Paradeplatz erfreut, stand neben einem begrenzten Raum im Untergeschoß ein Erdgeschoßraum mit relativ großer Raumhöhe zur Verfügung.
Die geforderte großzügige und elegante Warenpräsentation führte zum Einsatz von illusionistischen Mitteln, wobei den technischen Aspekten, wie Beleuchtung, Klimatisierung und Sicherheitseinrichtungen, sehr hohe Bedeutung zugemessen wurde.
Der optischen Vergrößerung des Hauptraums im Erdgeschoß dienen vor allem die

1. Plans (basement, ground floor, gallery floor).
2. View form outside into the shop. In front of the outer walls of the gallery large lighting elements are hung; these accentuate the high ceiling.
3. The salesroom in the basement.
4. The main room on the ground floor. The gallery with mirror plates on the outer surfaces contains a cool chamber in which the furs are stored.

1. Grundrisse (Untergeschoß, Erdgeschoß, Galeriegeschoß).
2. Blick von außen in das Geschäft. Vor den Außenwänden der Galerie hängen lange Leuchten, die die große Raumhöhe besonders betonen.
3. Der Verkaufsraum im Untergeschoß.
4. Der Hauptraum im Erdgeschoß. Das außen verspiegelte Galeriegeschoß enthält einen Kühlraum zum Lagern der Pelze.

Verspiegelungen der Außenflächen der Galerie sowie die vor dieser angebrachten Leuchten, deren Form die große Raumhöhe besonders betont.
Die Skala aus warmen Beigetönen, die mit den getönten und klaren Spiegeln ebenso harmoniert wie mit dem warmen Goldton der Messingbeschläge, schafft eine den kostbaren Pelzen angemessene Atmosphäre.

3

4

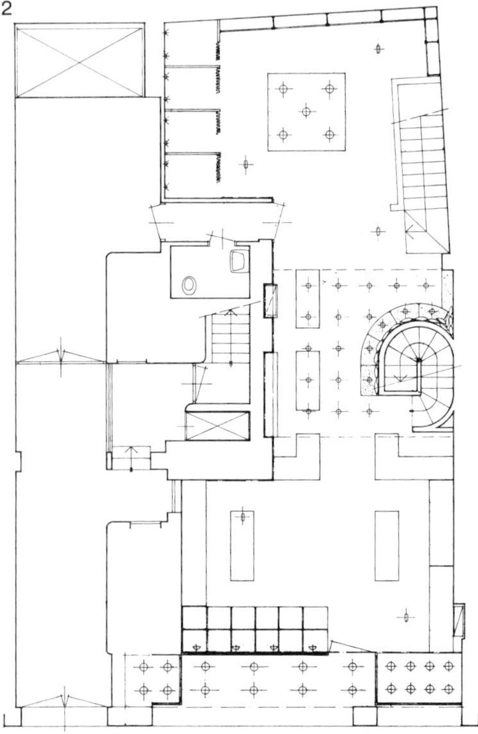

1

Krizia fashion shop, Milan
Architect: Piero Pinto

The main emphasis placed on the design of the Krizia fashion shop was the provision for an appropriate setting for the display and sale of the high-quality goods. Where new fashion is created, as here, attention should be focussed entirely on the colours and forms of the clothing on display; therefore the surroundings must remain as inconspicuous as possible.
With this in mind, the design of the entire arrangement was based on rigid, clear forms and uniform colours.

Modegeschäft Krizia, Mailand
Architekt: Piero Pinto

Beim Entwurf des Modegeschäfts Krizia kam es im wesentlichen darauf an, einen adäquaten Rahmen für die Zurschaustellung und den Verkauf der qualitativ sehr hochwertigen Waren zu schaffen. Wenn, wie an diesem Ort, eine neue Mode kreiert wird, soll die Umgebung so weit wie möglich zurücktreten, um die Aufmerksamkeit ganz auf die Farben und Formen der zur Schau gestellten Bekleidung zu richten.
Um dies zu erreichen, wurde die gesamte Einrichtung zum einen in strengen und reinen Formen und zum anderen in einem einheitlichen Farbton gehalten.

2

1. Because the shop front consists of a large area of glass, there is an unobstructed view into the interior of the shop.
2. Plan (ground floor).
3, 4. Salesroom. The design of the entire arrangement was based on rigid, clear forms and uniform colours so as to focus attention entirely on the clothes displayed.

1. Die Eingangsfront erlaubt durch ihre großflächige Verglasung einen ungehinderten Blick in das Ladeninnere.
2. Grundriß (Erdgeschoß).
3, 4. Verkaufsraum. Um die Aufmerksamkeit ganz auf die zur Schau gestellten Waren zu richten, wurde die gesamte Einrichtung in strengen und reinen Formen sowie in einem einheitlichen Farbton gehalten.

3

4

1. Axonometric view.
2. The effectiveness of the arrangement is achieved by display desks with transparent panes of glass running through the axis along the entire length and mirrors arranged directly above.

1. Axonometrie.
2. Der Haupteffekt der Einrichtung wird durch Schaupulte erzielt, bei denen über die ganze Länge in der Mittelachse durchsichtige Scheiben und darüber Spiegel angeordnet sind.

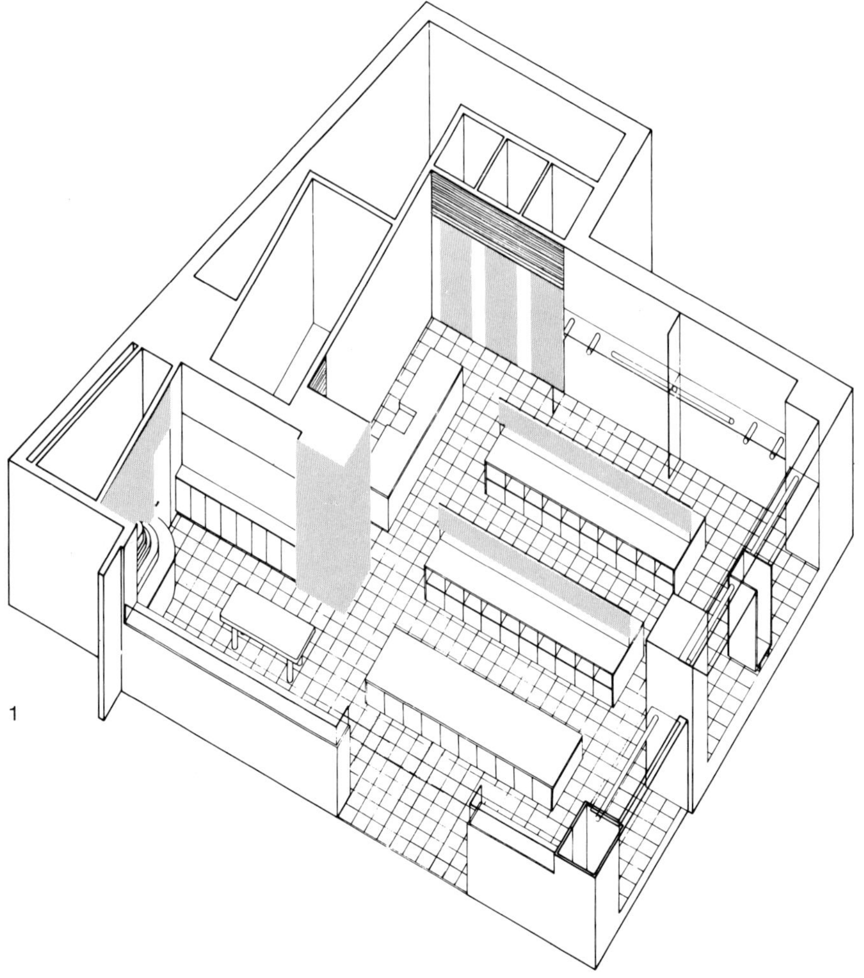

1

The Harajuku branch of the Takano fashion shop, Tokyo
Architects: Kuramata Design Office

The Harajuku branch of the Takano fashion shop is located on the first floor of the newly opened Harajuku-Le-Faure building. The effectiveness of the arrangement is achieved by display desks with transparent panes of glass running through the axis of the entire length and mirrors arranged directly above. Through the glass the visitor can overlook the area directly in front, while the mirror simultaneously provides him with a view to the rear.
The clarity and distinctiveness of the spatial layout is underlined by the precision in detail. The basic colouring is a combination of white and grey.

Harajuku-Filiale des Modegeschäfts Takano, Tokio
Architekten: Kuramata Design Office

Die Harajuku-Filiale des Modegeschäfts Takano befindet sich im 1. Obergeschoß des neu eröffneten Harajuku-Le-Faure-Gebäudes. Der Haupteffekt der Einrichtung wird durch Schaupulte erzielt, bei denen über die ganze Länge in der Mittellinie durchsichtige Scheiben und darüber Spiegel angeordnet sind; durch die Scheibe erblickt der Besucher den vor ihm liegenden Bereich, während ihm der Spiegel zugleich den Blick nach hinten gestattet.
Die überaus klare und übersichtliche räumliche Lösung wird durch die Präzision der Detaillösungen noch unterstrichen. Die Farbgebung beruht auf einer Kombination von Weiß und Grau.

INTERNATIONAL FASHION STORE
TAKANO
SHINJUKU · TOKYO

1. Plan. Key: 1 entrance, 2 counter, 3 store,
4 fitting room, 5 display.
2. View from the entrance into the salesroom.
3. The counter consists only of a thick veneered
table projecting out of the lateral light-metall
wall. Therefore it appears to hover over the floor.

1. Grundriß. Legende: 1 Eingang, 2 Verkaufstisch, 3 Lager, 4 Anproberaum, 5 Auslage.
2. Blick vom Eingang in den Verkaufsraum.
3. Der Verkaufstisch ist so konstruiert, daß
lediglich eine dicke furnierte Tischplatte frei aus
der seitlichen Leichtmetallwand auskragt und so
über dem Boden zu schweben scheint.

2

Issey Miyake boutique, Tokyo
Architect: Shiro Kuramata

The technical perfection and spatial concept of the Issey Miyake boutique would be inconceivable in a setting other than that of the classical Japanese house, in the rooms of which the centre of attention is the human being.
All-glass walls, which are separated only by a pier, open the salesroom visually on three sides. The remaining wall and the ceiling are covered with light metal; they are combined with display stands and cabinets in light wood, and very large mirrors. The counter consists only of a thick veneered table top projecting out of the lateral light-metal wall. Therefore it appears to hover over the floor.

Boutique Issey Miyake, Tokio
Architekt: Shiro Kuramata

Die Boutique Issey Miyake ist in ihrer technischen Perfektion und in ihrer Raumkonzeption nicht denkbar ohne das klassische japanische Haus, in dessen Räumen der Mensch als Mittelpunkt agiert.
Der Verkaufsraum öffnet sich optisch nach drei Seiten hin durch Ganzglaswände, die nur durch einen Pfeiler unterbrochen werden. Die verbleibenden Wandflächen und die Decke sind in Leichtmetall ausgeführt, kombiniert mit Stellagen und Schränken aus hellem Holz sowie großformatigen Spiegeln. Der Verkaufstisch ist so konstruiert, daß lediglich eine dicke furnierte Tischplatte frei aus der seitlichen Leichtmetallwand auskragt und so über dem Boden zu schweben scheint.

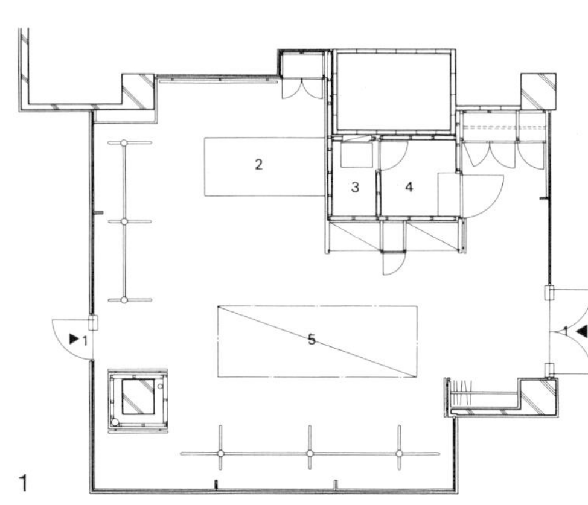

1

1. View from the entrance into the salesroom.
2. Salesroom. The furnishing system is built up on three units, comprising perforated sheets of steel painted white, cuboid shelf units with round edges, likewise in white, and tubular steel frames.

1. Blick vom Eingang in den Verkaufsraum.
2. Verkaufsraum. Das Ausbausystem baut auf drei Einheiten auf, auf gelochten, weiß lackierten Stahlplatten, ebenfalls in Weiß gehaltenen kubischen Regalelementen und Stahlrohrrahmen.

1

Polarn & Pyret children's fashion shop, Stockholm
Architects: Innovator Consult AB (Magnus Tengblad, Jan Dranger and Johan Huldt)

Polarn & Pyret is a chain of children's clothing shops specializing in high-quality material, first-class manufacture and good design.
The basic task of the architect was to provide a very simple, flexible system which could be applied throughout the room, but at the same time constituted an arrangement appropriate to the very specialized character and size of the articles to be displayed in this shop. The result is a system built up on three units, comprising perforated sheets of steel painted white, cuboid shelf units whith round edges, likewise in white, and tubular steel frames based on a module 90 cm or 40 cm wide and 145 cm high.
To facilitate orientation within the shop, it was decided to arrange the goods according to colour.

Kindermodengeschäft Polarn & Pyret, Stockholm
Architekten: Innovator Consult AB (Magnus Tengblad, Jan Dranger und Johan Huldt)

Polarn & Pyret ist eine Ladenkette für Kinderbekleidung, die auf hohe Qualität des Materials und der Verarbeitung sowie auf gutes Design spezialisiert ist.
Die Grundaufgabe der Architekten war, ein sehr einfaches, flexibles System zu finden, das über den gesamten Raum zu verwenden ist, das aber auch den sehr spezialisierten Artikeln und Größen dieses Geschäfts entspricht. Das Resultat ist ein System, das auf drei Einheiten aufbaut, bestehend aus gelochten, weiß lackierten Stahlplatten, ebenfalls in weiß gehaltenen kubischen Regalelementen mit runden Ecken und Stahlrohrrahmen, aufbauend auf einem Modul von 90 bzw. 45 cm Breite und 145 cm Höhe.
Die Überlegungen zur Farbgebung gingen dahin, die Waren nach Farben zusammenzufassen. Das gibt dem Raum ein einfaches »Farbmaß«, das die Orientierung erleichtert.

barn
9-14
år
baby
Musse kläder
Musse kläder
BOMULLS-
POLO
20:-
TRÖJA
15:-
20:-

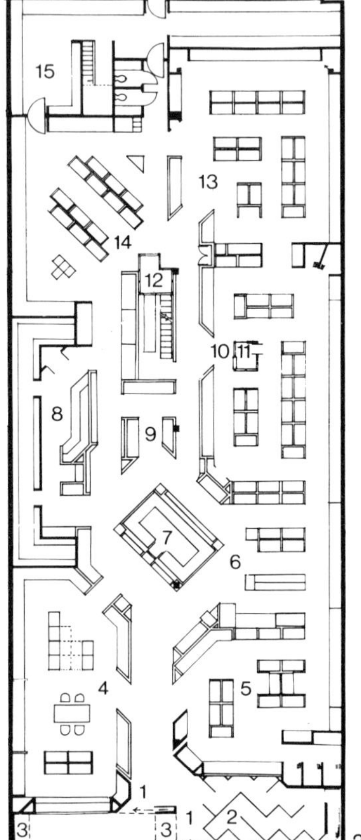

1

The Children's Place children's fashion and toy shop, Willowbrook Center, Wayne Township, New Jersey
Architects: George Nelson & Company

A shop which caters exclusively for children should take into consideration the preferences, the psychic attitude and the physical capabilities of the children. The design of The Children's Place was based on this premise. The flags and cylinders suspended from the ceiling to indicate the individual departments, as well as the toys and articles of clothing attached to pipes, give the shop a deliberately playful, almost circus-like character. Moreover, one fifth of the floor area is reserved as playing areas where the children can have fun with play-houses, slides, tunnels, labyrinths and distorting mirrors, while their mothers are otherwise occupied.

Kindermoden- und Spielwarengeschäft The Children's Place, Willowbrook Center, Wayne Township, New Jersey
Architekten: George Nelson & Company

Dem Design des Geschäfts The Children's Place lag das Ziel zugrunde, bei der Gestaltung eines Ladens, in dem Waren für Kinder verkauft werden, so weit wie möglich auf deren Neigungen, psychische Einstellung und physische Möglichkeiten einzugehen. So geben herunterhängende Fahnen und Zylinder, die die einzelnen Abteilungen markieren, sowie in einem Rohrsystem befestigte Kleidungsstücke und Spielwaren dem Laden einen bewußt spielerischen, fast zirkushaften Charakter. Darüber hinaus wurde ein Fünftel der Ladenfläche für Spielzonen reserviert, wo sich die Kinder mit Spielhäusern, Rutschen, Tunnels, Labyrinthen und Spiegel-Kabinetten vergnügen können, während die Mütter anderweitig beschäftigt sind.

1. Entrance front. The large shop-window is divided by a closed band in an upper section for adults and older children, and in a lower section for younger children.
2. Plan. Key: 1 entrance, 2 maze, 3 show case, 4 play area for infants, 5 older girls, 6 accessories, 7 cash desk and wrapping counter, 8 shoes, 9 special sales, 10 younger girls, 11 play house, 12 play tower, 13 boys, 14 toys, 15 store.
3. View from the entrance area into the interior of the shop.
4. Cash desk and wrapping counter. The convex mirrors in the lower section are to amuse waiting children.

1. Eingangsfront. Das große Schaufenster ist durch ein geschlossenes Band in eine obere Zone für Erwachsene und ältere Kinder und eine untere Zone für jüngere Kinder geteilt.
2. Grundriß. Legende: 1 Eingang, 2 Irrgarten, 3 Vitrine, 4 Spielzone für Kleinkinder, 5 ältere Mädchen, 6 Accessoires, 7 Kasse und Packtisch, 8 Schuhe, 9 Sonderverkauf, 10 jüngere Mädchen, 11 Spielhaus, 12 Spielturm, 13 Knaben, 14 Spielzeug, 15 Lager.
3. Blick vom Eingangsbereich in das Ladeninnere.
4. Kasse und Packtisch. Die konvexen Spiegel im unteren Bereich dienen der Belustigung wartender Kinder.

3

4

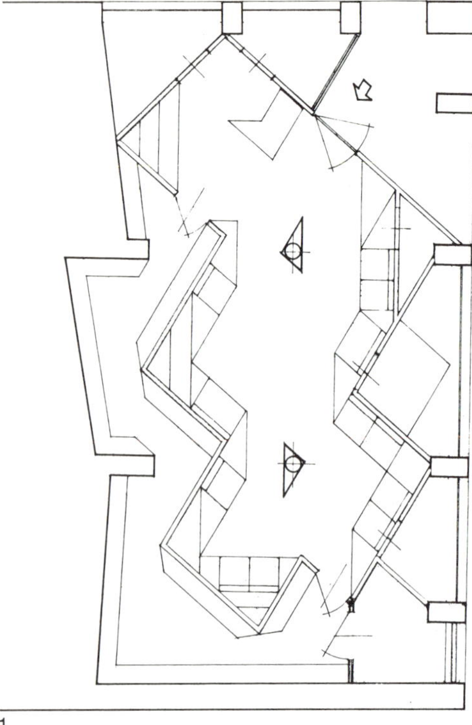

1

2

3

4

1. Plan.
2–4. Salesroom. The floor plan and form of the shop are based on a diagonal. The resulting triangle dominates the entire shop interior, including the encasement of the columns.
5. The shop front showing to the Campo S. Salvador. On the right the covered entrance.

1. Grundriß.
2–4. Verkaufsraum. Für Grundriß und Form des Geschäfts wurde die Diagonale gewählt. Die dadurch entstandene Dreiecksform bestimmt den ganzen Innenraum bis hin zur Verkleidung der Säulen.
5. Die Ladenfront zum Campo S. Salvador. Rechts der gedeckte Eingangsbereich.

5

Rossetti shoe shop, Venice
Architect: Piero Pinto

The Rossetti company's shoe shops are all built along similar lines, whereby the distribution of space is determined as follows: one third for displayed merchandise, a little less than one third for the sales area and the rest for stock.
After studying the behaviour of passers-by and ascertaining the necessary position and size of the showcases on the street, the showcases and the entrance were placed in such a way that there is a covered entrance on the corner of the Campo S. Salvador and the Via Mazzani. The floor plan and form of the shop are based on a diagonal. The resulting triangle dominates the entire shop interior, including the encasement of the columns. The customers' seating, arranged along the partitioning walls, offers an unobstructed view of the merchandise, which is openly displayed on pedestals on various levels.

Schuhgeschäft Rossetti, Venedig
Architekt: Piero Pinto

Die Schuhläden der Firma Rossetti sind alle nach ähnlichen Prinzipien errichtet, wobei die Aufteilung der Räume etwa nach folgendem Schlüssel erfolgt: ein Drittel für die Auslagen, etwas weniger als ein Drittel für den Verkauf und der Rest für das Lager.
Nach dem Studium des Verhaltens der Passanten und der erforderlichen Lage und Größe der Vitrinen an der Straße wurden die Auslagen und der Eingang so gelegt, daß an der Ecke des Campo S. Salvador und der Via Mazzini ein gedeckter Eingang entstand. Für Grundriß und Form des Geschäfts wurde die Diagonale gewählt. Die dadurch entstandene Dreiecksform bestimmt den gesamten Innenraum bis hin zur Verkleidung der Säulen. Entlang der raumtrennenden Wände wurden die Sitzplätze für die Kunden so angeordnet, daß die Waren frei stehend auf Podesten in verschiedenen Höhen, im nahen Umkreis der Kunden, zur Schaustellung gelangen.

1

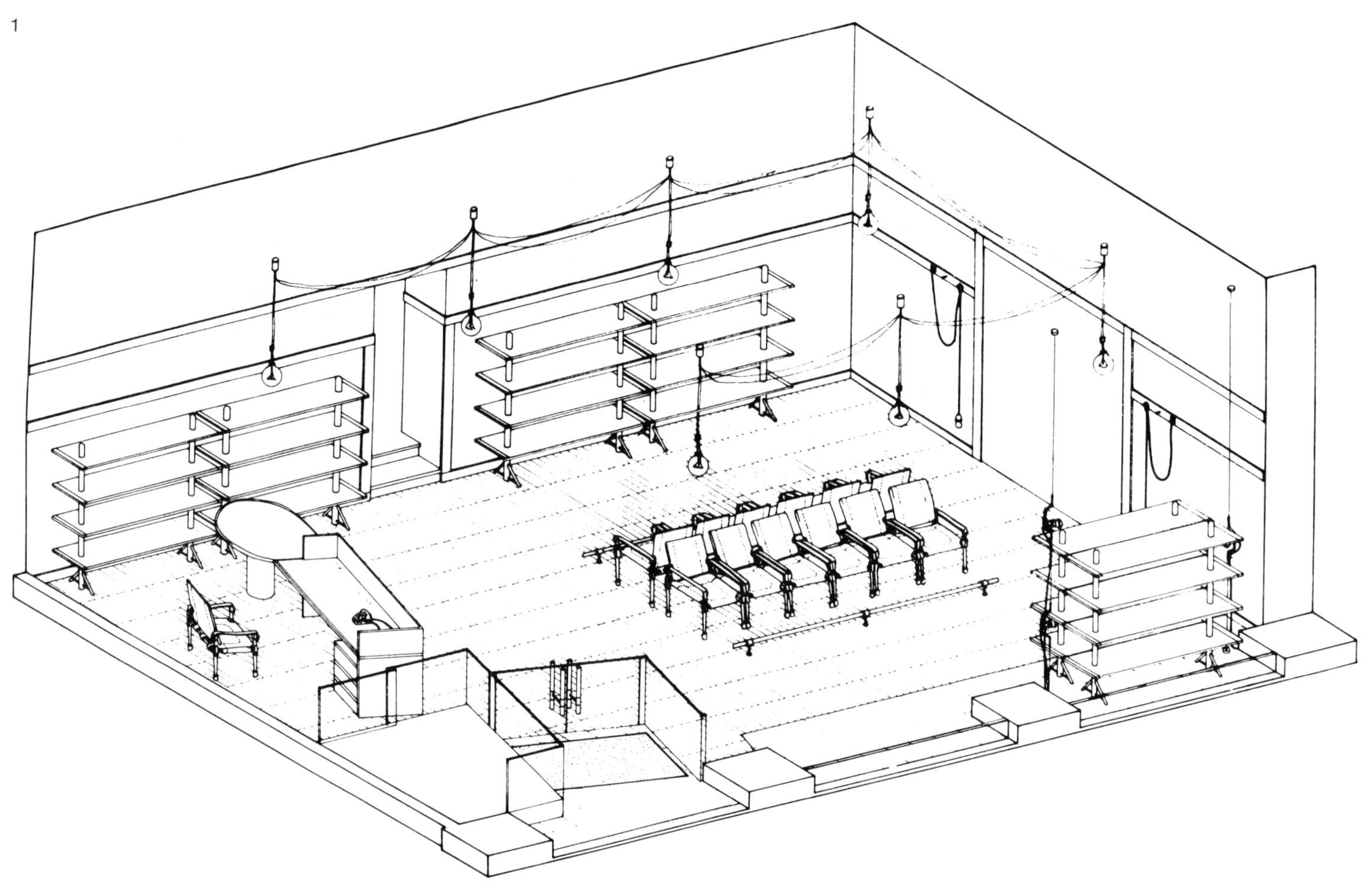

La Skarpa shoe shop, Casala Monferrato, Italy
Architect: Antonio Rossin

A betting shop with an area of 60 m² in the old town centre of Casala Monferrato was converted into a shoe shop for young people. The small area, the limited resources and the tight building schedule ruled out an extravagant formal design, restricting the conversion to the mere fulfillment of the essential requirements.
The shop-windows give a view into the shop interior, transforming the entire shop into an open display. The reflection of the interior in a large mirror on the front wall gives the impression that an identical room exists directly behind.

Schuhgeschäft La Skarpa, Casale Monferrato, Italien
Architekt: Antonio Rossin

Im alten Stadtzentrum von Casale Monferrato wurde ein Wettbüro mit einer Grundfläche von etwa 60 m² in ein Schuhgeschäft für Jugendliche umgewandelt. Die kleine Fläche, die geringen zur Verfügung stehenden Mittel und eine knappe Bauzeit erlaubten keine aufwendige formale Gestaltung, sondern nötigten dazu, sich auf das Wesentliche der Aufgabe zu beschränken.
Die Auslagen geben den Blick in das Innere des Geschäfts frei, der gesamte Laden wurde so zu einer durchgehenden Ausstellung. Zudem spiegelt sich der gesamte Innenraum in einem großen, an der Stirnseite angebrachten Spiegel, so daß der Eindruck erweckt wird, der Raum sei dahinter noch einmal vorhanden.

2

3

4

1. Axonometric view.
2. View from outside into the salesroom.
3. The entrance area, seen from inside.
4. The display stand is designed in such a way that it does not obstruct the view from outside into the interior of the shop.
5. Salesroom. The limited resources ruled out an extravagant formal design, restricting the conversion to the mere fulfillment of the essential requirements.

1. Axonometrie.
2. Blick von außen in den Verkaufsraum.
3. Der Eingangsbereich von innen.
4. Das Auslagengestell ist so gestaltet, daß es den Blick von außen in das Innere des Ladens nicht behindert.
5. Verkaufsraum. Die geringen zur Verfügung stehenden Mittel erlaubten keine aufwendige formale Gestaltung, sondern nötigten dazu, sich auf das Wesentliche zu beschränken.

5

1

2

Ciro jewellery shop, Vienna
Architect: Carl Auböck

This shop, on the Graben, belongs to a sales organisation which operates both in Europe and overseas, and was planned as a prototype. The design of the other shops is based on this model, whereby each one has individual characteristics which suit local conditions. The recessed entrance and small showcases with their attractive display of jewellery invite passers-by to linger, and the curved panes of glass give an excellent view into the shop interior. The illuminated lettering, an integral part of the shop front, stands out against the background and its light is reflected to the rear. The single tables for private sales discussions are important elements of the interior furnishing.

Perlen-Fachgeschäft Ciro, Wien
Architekt: Carl Auböck

Der am Graben liegende Laden gehört zu einer sowohl in Europa als auch in Übersee operierenden Verkaufsorganisation und wurde als Prototyp geplant. Die weiteren Läden entstanden in Anlehnung daran, wobei die örtlichen Gegebenheiten zu unterschiedlichen Ausprägungen führten.
Der zurückgesetzte Eingang und kleine Schmuckvitrinen fordern zum Verweilen auf, gekurvte Scheiben erleichtern den Einblick in das Geschäft. Integrierter Bestandteil der Front ist die nach rückwärts leuchtende und sich vom Hintergrund abhebende Schrift. Wesentliche Elemente der Möblierung des Innenraums sind die Einzeltische für persönliche Verkaufsgespräche.

3

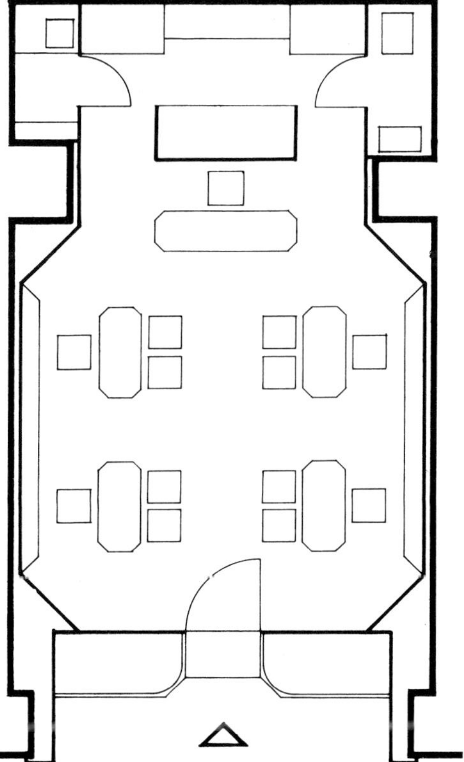

4

5

6

7

1. Entrance front.
2, 3. Salesroom. The single tables for private sales discussions are important elements of the interior furnishing.
4. Plan.
5. The entrance front of the Ciro shop in Frankfurt.
6. The entrance front of the Ciro shop in Düsseldorf.
7. The entrance front of the Ciro shop in Cologne.

1. Eingangsfront.
2, 3. Verkaufsraum. Wesentliche Elemente der Möblierung sind die Einzeltische für persönliche Verkaufsgespräche.
4. Grundriß.
5. Die Eingangsfront des Ciro-Geschäfts in Frankfurt.
6. Die Eingangsfront des Ciro-Geschäfts in Düsseldorf.
7. Die Eingangsfront des Ciro-Geschäfts in Köln.

1

Parodi jewellery shop, Genoa
Architect: Gianfranco Frattini

The Parodi jewellery shop is accommodated in the rooms of a former bank, and a part of
the security system, namely the strong-room in the basement, has been retained.
The floor in one part of the shop has been raised to form an area where, when seated,
a customer can remain unobserved by passers-by. The sale of jewellery and precious
stones is undertaken in the former strong-room which has been converted into
a salesroom.
The walls are lined with camel-coloured cloth, the ceiling with dark-brown cloth, and the
floor has beige-coloured carpeting. The showcases are lined with dark red leather, and the
metal and coloured elements are painted dark-green.

Juweliergeschäft Parodi, Genua
Architekt: Gianfranco Frattini

Das Juweliergeschäft Parodi wurde in die Räumlichkeiten einer ehemaligen Bank
eingebaut, von der ein Teil des Sicherheitssystems, nämlich der Tresorraum im
Untergeschoß, übernommen wurde.
In einem Teil des Geschäfts wurde der Fußboden angehoben, um einen Bereich zu bilden,
in dem der Kunde, wenn er sitzt, nicht von Straßenpassanten beobachtet werden kann.
Der Verkauf von Juwelen oder besonderen Steinen erfolgt im ehemaligen Tresorraum, der
zu einem Verkaufsraum umgestaltet wurde.
Die Wände sind mit kamelfarbenem Tuch überzogen, die Decke mit dunkelbraunem Tuch;
als Bodenbelag dient ein beigefarbener Teppich. Das Innere der Ausstellungsvitrinen ist
mit dunkelrotem Leder verkleidet, die Metallteile und die farbigen Teile sind dunkelgrün
lackiert.

1, 2. The floor in one part of the ground-floor room has been raised to form an area where, when seated, a customer can remain unobserved by passers-by.
3. The lower part of the ground-floor room.
4. Plan (ground floor).

1, 2. In einem Teil des Erdgeschoßraumes wurde der Boden angehoben, um einen Bereich zu bilden, in dem der Kunde, wenn er sitzt, nicht von Straßenpassanten beobachtet werden kann.
3. Der untere Teil des Erdgeschoßraumes.
4. Grundriß (Erdgeschoß).

2

3
4

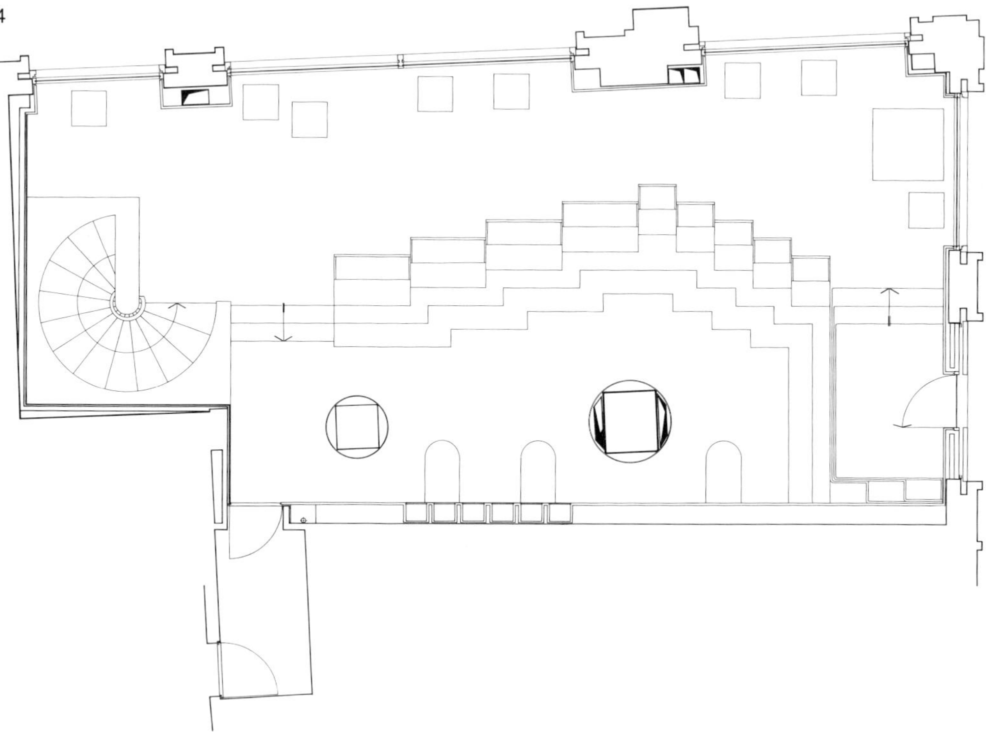

2

1

Asprey & Co. Ltd. jewellery shop, London
Architects: Gordon Bowyer & Partners

The new display and salesrooms of Asprey & Co. Ltd. are housed on the ground floor and first floor of what was formerly a private residence. It adjoins Asprey's business premises in Bond Street, to which it is connected by a lift. Access to the rooms is gained from Grafton Street, where new entrances have been built, and from Bond Street by means of an L-shaped staircase.
Articles of jewellery, displayed in showcases, are sold on the ground floor. Specially designed sales counters (where the customer is served while seated) as well as the choice of materials, the colouring of which has been restricted to a minimum, guarantee an atmosphere of privacy. For security reasons, mirrors and television cameras fitted on a level with the showcases monitor the entire room.
Diamonds and other precious stones are sold on the first floor. The sales counters in this area are screened off by semicircular wooden partitions, approximatley 1,40 m high, which permit a view from the inside to the outside but obstruct the view from the outside. Privileged customers are served in a separate room which can be closed off by a sliding door.

Juweliergeschäft Asprey & Co. Ltd., London
Architekten: Gordon Bowyer & Partners

Die neuen Schau- und Verkaufsräume von Asprey & Co. Ltd. wurden im Erdgeschoß und im 1. Obergeschoß eines ehemaligen Privathauses eingerichtet, das an Aspreys Geschäftsräume in der Bond Street anschließt und von dort mit einem Aufzug zu erreichen ist. Durch neu geschaffene Eingänge sind die Räume von der Grafton Street und – über eine L-förmige Treppe – auch von der Bond Street zugänglich.
Im Erdgeschoß werden Schmuckstücke verkauft, die in Vitrinen zur Schau gestellt sind. Besonders entworfene Verkaufspulte, an denen der Kunde sitzend bedient wird,

1. View of the reception desk through the Bond Street entrance.
2. View from inside towards the Grafton Street entrance.
3. The salesroom on the ground floor. Here articles of jewellery displayed in showcases are sold.
4. Plans (ground floor, upper floor). Key: 1 entrance from Grafton Street, 2 entrance from Bond Street.

1. Blick durch den Eingang von der Bond Street auf den Empfang.
2. Blick von innen auf den Eingang von der Grafton Street.
3. Der Verkaufsraum im Erdgeschoß. Hier werden Schmuckstücke verkauft, die in Vitrinen zur Schau gestellt sind.
4. Grundrisse (Erdgeschoß, Obergeschoß). Legende: 1 Eingang von der Grafton Street, 2 Eingang von der Bond Street.

3

gewährleisten ebenso eine private Atmosphäre wie die Wahl der verwendeten Materialien, die sich auf ein Minimum von Farben beschränken. Für Sicherheit sorgen in Vitrinenhöhe angeordnete Spiegel und Fernsehkameras, die den ganzen Raum überwachen.
Im 1. Obergeschoß werden Diamanten und andere wertvolle Edelsteine verkauft. Die Verkaufspulte in diesem Bereich sind von halbkreisförmigen, etwa 1,40 m hohen Holzverkleidungen umgeben, die wohl den Blick von innen nach außen gestatten, den Einblick von außen aber verwehren. Ein durch eine Schiebetür verschließbarer Raum dient dem Verkauf an bevorzugte Kunden.

4

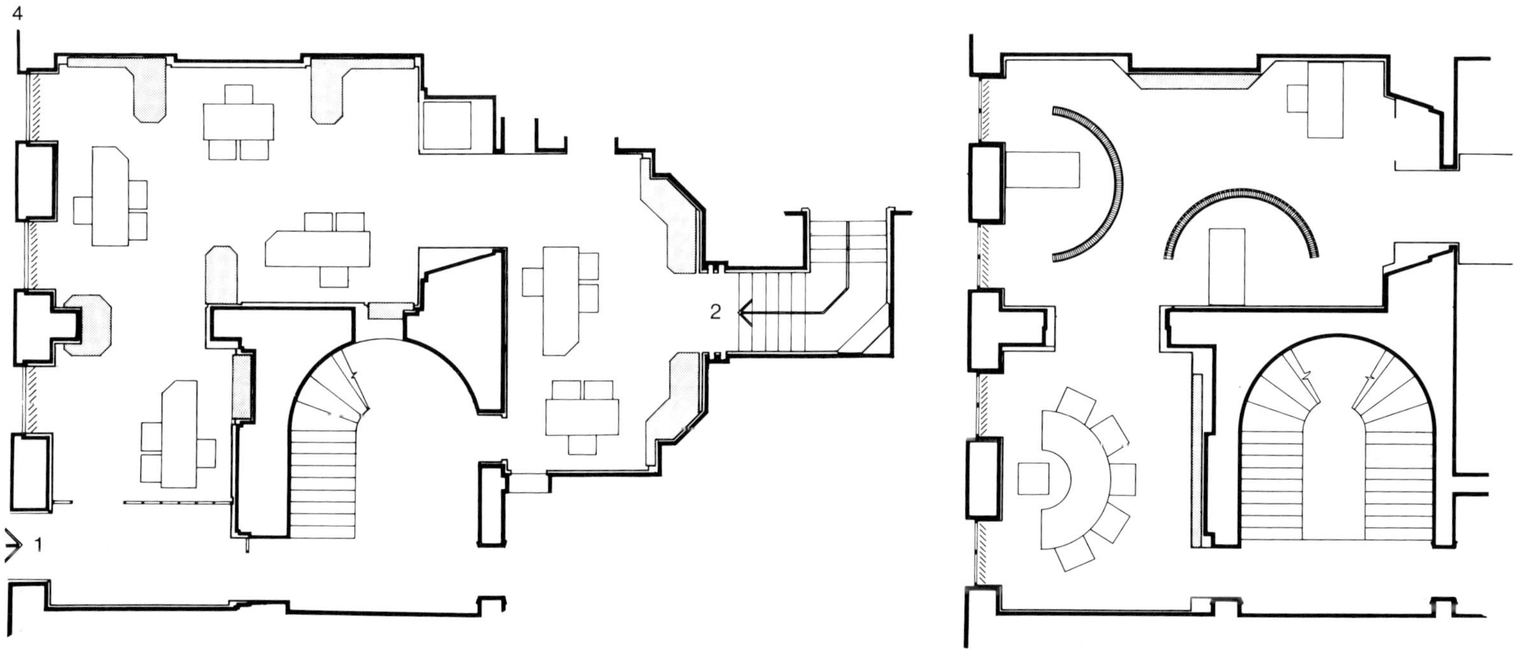

5

6

5, 6. The salesrooms on the upper floor. This is where diamonds are sold. The sales counters are screened off by semicircular wooden partitions, which permit a view from the inside to the outside but obstruct the view from the outside.

5, 6. Der Verkaufsraum im Obergeschoß. Hier werden Diamanten verkauft. Die Verkaufspulte sind von halbkreisförmigen Holzverkleidungen umgeben, die wohl den Blick von innen nach außen gestatten, den Einblick von außen aber verwehren.

1, 2. Entrance front. Fresh air goes through the laminae in the "break" in the façade, stale air comes out through the pipes. The materials applied include blackish-brown granite, brass and stainless steel.

1, 2. Eingangsfront. Durch die Lamellen in dem Fassaden-»Bruch« wird die Zuluft geführt, durch die Rohre die Abluft. Die verwendeten Materialien sind schwarzbrauner Granit, Messing und rostfreier Stahl.

1

2

Schullin jewellery shop, Vienna
Architect: Hans Hollein

The formal concept of the Schullin jewellery shop on the Graben is closely linked with its size. With a limited façade area and a interior no larger than 13.5 m² a well-thought out use of resources was necessary, while, on the other hand, scope for details and materials of an exceptionally high quality, even for a shop of this type, was allowed.
Prompted by the select character of the neighbourhood – the Graben is regarded as one of the most elegant shopping areas in Vienna – and of the shop itself, the architect has placed the accent of design on exclusiveness, extravagance even, and in so doing has ventured into the sphere of art. The materials applied include blackish-brown granite, brass in a variety of shades and stainless steel outside, and additionally, brown velvet, leather and cherrywood inside. The visual enlargement of the tiny room is effected by mirrors.

Juweliergeschäft Schullin, Wien
Architekt: Hans Hollein

Die gestalterische Konzeption des am Graben gelegenen Juweliergeschäfts Schullin steht in engem Zusammenhang mit seiner Dimension. Die kleine Fassadenfläche und ein Innenraum mit einer Größe von nicht mehr als 13,5 m² machten einen äußerst überlegten Einsatz der Mittel zur Voraussetzung, erlaubten auf der anderen Seite jedoch eine auch für ein Geschäft dieser Art überdurchschnittlich hohe Material- und Detailqualität.

Das Niveau der Umgebung – der Graben zählt zu den elegantesten Einkaufsbereichen Wiens – und auch das Geschäft selbst veranlaßte den Architekten, einen exklusiven, ja extravaganten Ton anzuschlagen und dabei bis in den rein künstlerischen Bereich vorzustoßen. Die verwendeten Materialien sind außen schwarzbrauner Granit, verschieden getöntes Messing und rostfreier Stahl sowie innen zusätzlich brauner Samt, Leder und Kirschholz. Spiegel sorgen dafür, daß der winzige Raum optisch erweitert wird.

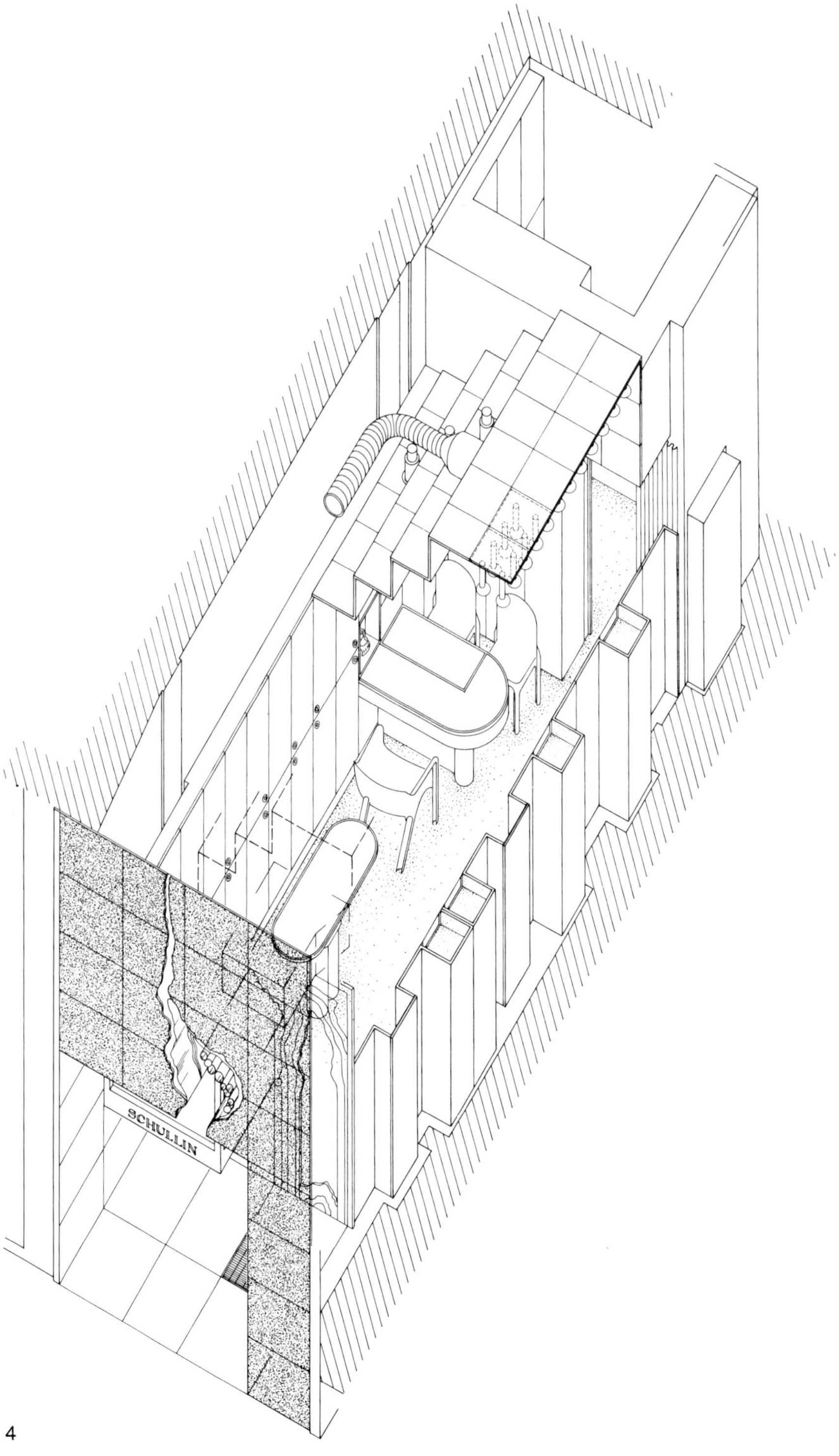

3

3. The salesroom, looking towards the entrance. In addition to the materials used outside, brown velvet, leather and cherrywood were used inside.
4. Axonometric view.
5. Detail of the entrance wall from inside.

3. Der Verkaufsraum in Richtung Eingang. Zu den außen verwendeten Materialien kommen hier noch brauner Samt, Leder und Kirschholz hinzu.
4. Axonometrie.
5. Detail der Eingangswand von innen.

4

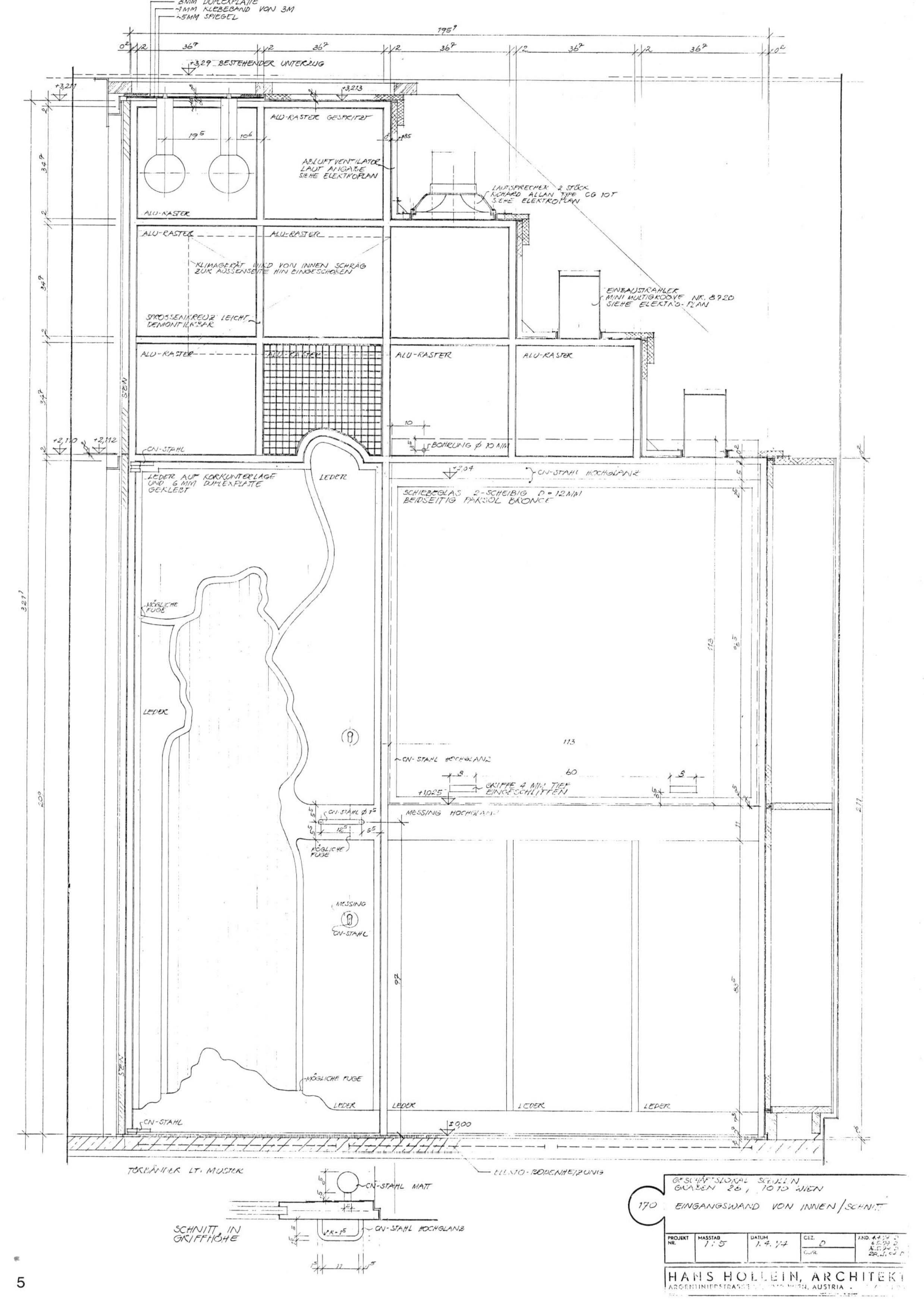
8MM DUPLEXPLATTE
~7MM KLEBEBAND VON 3M
~5MM SPIEGEL
+3,29 BESTEHENDER UNTERZUG
ALU-RASTER GESPRITZT
ABLUFTVENTILATOR
LAUT ANGABE
SIEHE ELEKTROPLAN
LAUTSPRECHER 2 STÜCK
RICHARD ALLAN TYPE CG 10T
SIEHE ELEKTROPLAN
ALU-RASTER
ALU-RASTER
ALU-RASTER
KLIMAGERÄT WIRD VON INNEN SCHRÄG
ZUR AUSSENSEITE HIN EINGESCHOBEN
EINBAUSTRAHLER
MINI MULTIGROOVE NR. 8720
SIEHE ELEKTRO-PLAN
SPROSSENKREUZ LEICHT
DEMONTIERBAR
ALU-RASTER
ALU-RASTER
ALU-RASTER
BOHRUNG ⌀ 10 MM
CN-STAHL
CN-STAHL HOCHGLANZ
LEDER AUF KORKUNTERLAGE
UND 6MM DUPLEXPLATTE
GEKLEBT
LEDER
SCHIEBEGLAS 2-SCHEIBIG D = 12MM
BEIDSEITIG PARSOL BRONCE
MÖGLICHE
FUGE
LEDER
CN-STAHL HOCHGLANZ
GRIFFE 4 MM TIEF
EINGESCHNITTEN
CN-STAHL ⌀ 1
MESSING HOCHGLANZ
MÖGLICHE
FUGE
MESSING
CN-STAHL
MÖGLICHE FUGE
LEDER
LEDER
LEDER
LEDER
CN-STAHL
TÜRRÄNDER LT. MUSTER
LENTO-BODENHEIZUNG
CN-STAHL MATT
CN-STAHL HOCHGLANZ
SCHNITT IN
GRIFFHÖHE
GESCHÄFTSLOKAL SCHULLIN
GRABEN 26, 1010 WIEN
170 EINGANGSWAND VON INNEN / SCHNITT
PROJEKT NR.
MASSTAB 1:5
DATUM 1.4.74
GEZ. D
HANS HOLLEIN, ARCHITEKT
ARGENTINIERSTRASSE, 1040 WIEN, AUSTRIA

1

Synpunkten optician's shop, Stockholm
Architects: Innovator Consult AB (Magnus Tengblad)

The normal optician's shop in Sweden is very small and offers only a limited selection of goods. In the Synpunkten optician's shop, on the other hand, customers can choose from 5000 different spectacles.
Ladies' and men's spectacles, as well as spectacles for sports, are all displayed separately and within these categories are arranged according to steel frames, plastic frames etc. Three different price categories are fixed by a colour code. A box with four compartments stands in the room to give customers the opportunity to try on the frames without being disturbed.
The room itself is a concrete construction. The mechanical equipment includes a simple ventilation system of galvanized pipes with a lighting system fitted directly below. A rubber finish was chosen for the floor.

Optikergeschäft Synpunkten, Stockholm
Architekten: Innovator Consult AB (Magnus Tengblad)

Der übliche Optikerladen in Schweden ist sehr klein, und entsprechend bescheiden ist dort auch das Angebot. Im Gegensatz hierzu hat der Kunde in dem Optikergeschäft Synpunkten die Auswahl unter 5000 verschiedenen Brillen.
Damen-, Herren- und Sportbrillen werden gesondert ausgestellt, darüber hinaus erfolgt eine Einteilung nach Fassungen aus Stahl, Kunststoff usw. Ein Farbencode legt drei verschiedene Preiskategorien fest. Eine frei im Raum angeordnete Box mit vier Kojen gibt den Kunden die Möglichkeit, die Fassungen ungestört anzuprobieren.
Der Raum selbst ist eine Betonkonstruktion. Ein einfaches System für die Lüftung aus galvanisierten Rohren mit darunterliegendem Beleuchtungssystem bildet die technische Einrichtung. Für den Boden wurde ein Gummibelag gewählt.

1. View into the display area. The spectacle
frames are fixed on large boards.
2. Plan. Key: 1 entrance, 2 cash desk, 3 display
area, 4 fitting cubicle.
3. Cashier area.
4. View into a fitting cubicle.

1. Blick in den Ausstellungsbereich. Die Brillen
sind auf großen Tafeln befestigt.
2. Grundriß. Legende: 1 Eingang, 2 Kasse,
3 Ausstellungsbereich, 4 Anprobekoje.
3. Kassenbereich.
4. Blick in eine Anprobekoje.

3

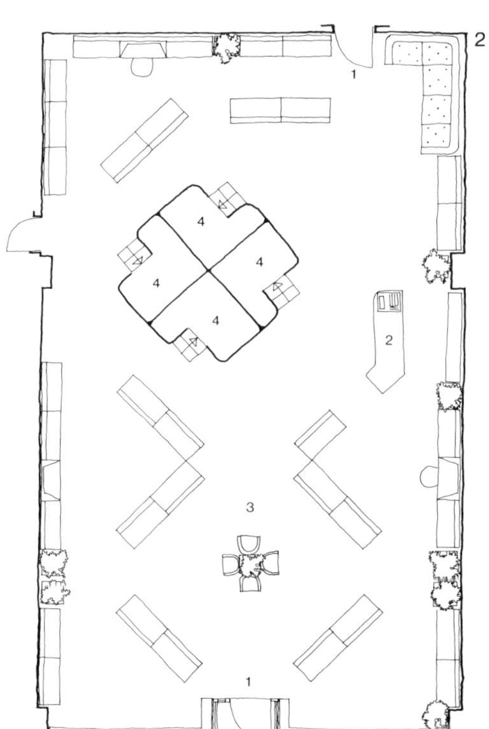

2

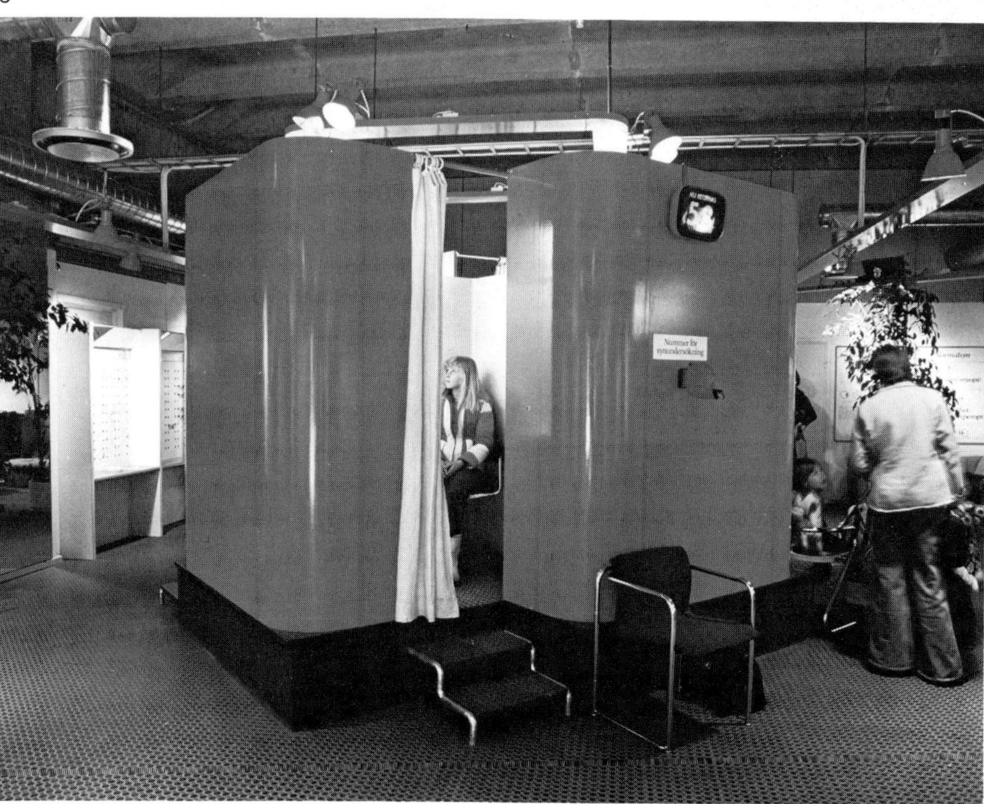

4

1

Vidal Sassoon hairdressing salon, San Francisco
Architects: Gordon Bowyer & Partners

The hairdressing salons of the Vidal Sassoon company, which are to be found in the largest cities of England and America, all follow the same principle. Contrary to customary practice in this field, reception rooms as well as work rooms are made visible to passer-by through wide-open glass fronts. The technical accentuation of the interior design itself owes its origin to the formal language of the International Style.
One of these salons is accommodated in a late 19th century building on Grant Avenue in San Francisco. A typical feature of the façade is not only the extensive glazing and the delicate cast-iron construction but above all the external fire-escape. The transparent front which allows a view into the salon forms an integral part of this façade.
The salon is equipped for both ladies' and gentlemen's hairdressing.

Frisiersalon Vidal Sassoon, San Francisco
Architekten: Gordon Bowyer & Partners

Die Frisiersalons der Firma Vidal Sassoon, die in den wichtigsten Städten Englands und Amerikas zu finden sind, gehorchen alle den gleichen Prinzipien. Empfangsräume, aber auch Arbeitsräume werden im Gegensatz zu den Gepflogenheiten dieser Branche durch weit geöffnete Glasfronten dem Passanten sichtbar gemacht. Die Einrichtung selbst ist in ihrer betont technischen Grundhaltung der Formensprache des Internationalen Stils verpflichtet.
Einer dieser Salons wurde an der Grant Avenue in San Francisco in einem Gebäude aus dem späten 19. Jahrhundert eingerichtet. Typisch für die Fassade ist nicht nur die großflächige Verglasung und die feingliedrige Gußeisenkonstruktion, sondern vor allem auch die außen gelegene Feuertreppe. Die durchsichtig gehaltene Front mit dem Einblick in das Innere des Salons ordnet sich dieser Fassade fast nahtlos ein.
Der Salon ist für Damen- und Herrenbedienung eingerichtet.

1. Contrary to customary practice in this field, the reception rooms as well as the work rooms of Vidal Sassoon are made visible to passers-by through wide-open glass fronts.
2. View of the 19th century building from Grant Avenue.

1. Im Gegensatz zu den Gepflogenheiten der Branche werden Empfangs- und Arbeitsräume bei der Firma Vidal Sassoon durch weit geöffnete Glasfronten dem Passanten sichtbar gemacht.
2. Ansicht des aus dem 19. Jahrhundert stammenden Gebäudes von der Grant Avenue.

2

3. Plans (ground floor, upper floor) and section.
Key: 1 reception, 2 advance appointment,
3 changing room, 4 coats, 5 work stations for
ladies, 6 waiting area, 7 dryers, 8 shampoo
stations, 9 store, 10 dispensary, 11 existing stair
and lift lobby, 12 private cubicles, 13 tinting and
tricology, 14 clients' lavatory, 15 staff lavatory, 16
existing office, 17 work stations for men.
4. The salon on the ground floor, seen from the
entrance area.
5. The salon on the ground floor, looking towards the entrance area.
6, 7. Work stations for ladies.

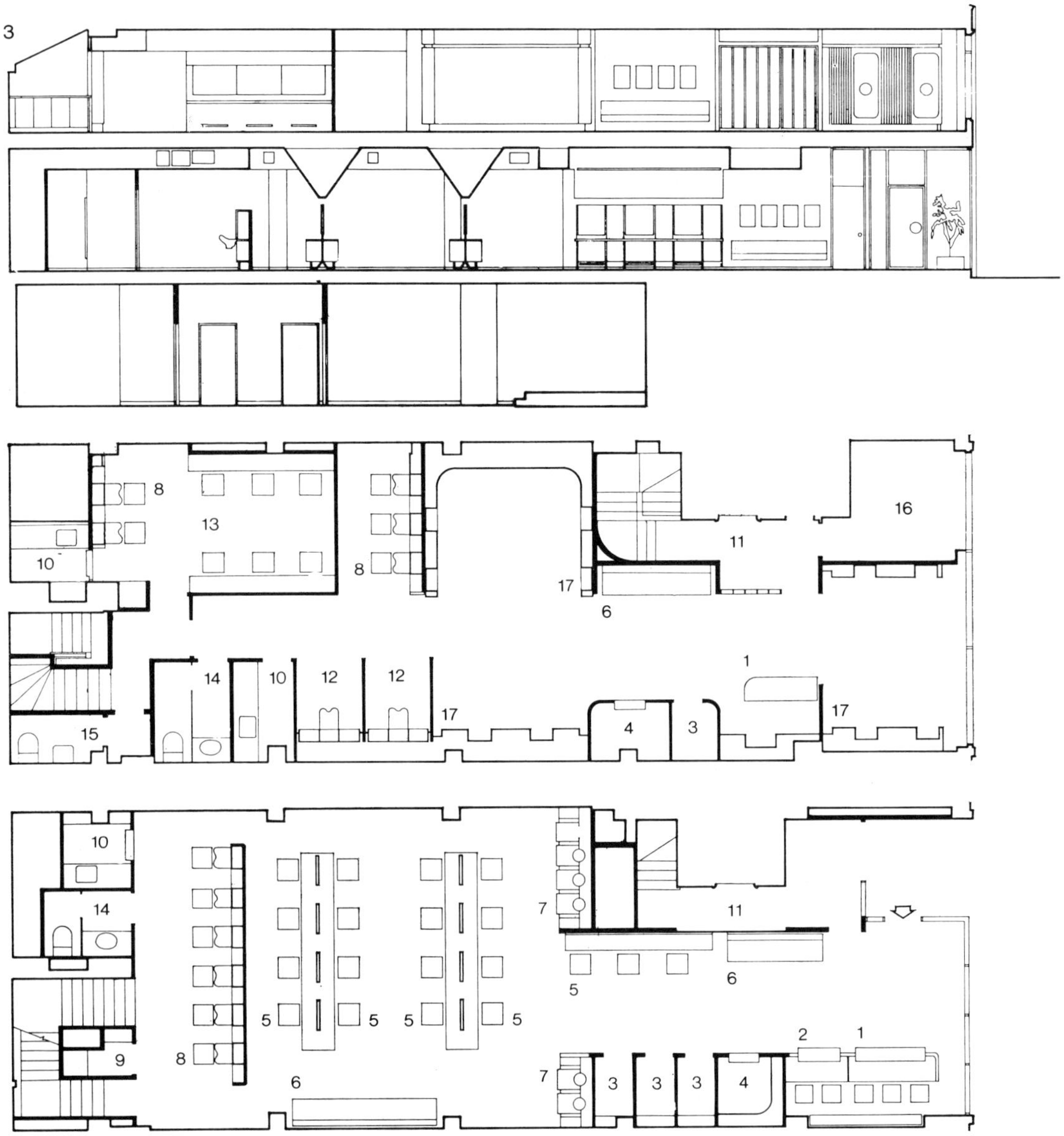

3. Grundrisse (Erdgeschoß, Obergeschoß) und Schnitt. Legende: 1 Empfang, 2 Voranmeldung, 3 Umkleide, 4 Mäntel, 5 Kundenplätze für Damen, 6 Warteplätze, 7 Trockner, 8 Schampunierplätze, 9 Lager, 10 Apotheke, 11 bestehende Treppe und Aufzugslobby, 12 Einzelkabinen, 13 Färben und Tönen, 14 Kunden-WC, 15 Personal-WC, 16 bestehendes Büro, 17 Kundenplätze für Herren.
4. Der Salon im Erdgeschoß vom Eingangsbereich aus gesehen.
5. Der Salon im Erdgeschoß in Richtung Eingangsbereich gesehen.
6, 7. Kundenplätze für Damen.

1

2

Vidal Sassoon hairdressing salon, Manchester
Architects: Gordon Bowyer & Partners

As in San Francisco, the hairdressing salon of the Vidal Sassoon company in Manchester is accommodated in a 19th century house, and the salon interior is here too visible from the street through a glass front. The ladies' hairdressing rooms are located on the ground and first floor, the gentlemen's salon is in the basement.
While ceilings and supports have been retained in their original condition, the entire interior arrangement is modern. The new lamps and air-conditioning ducts hang at a considerable distance below the old ceilings.

Frisiersalon Vidal Sassoon, Manchester
Architekten: Gordon Bowyer & Partners

Wie in San Francisco wurde auch in Manchester der Frisiersalon der Firma Vidal Sassoon in einem Haus aus dem 19. Jahrhundert eingerichtet. Ebenso wurde hier das Innere des Salons von der Straße her durch eine Glasfront sichtbar gemacht. Im Erdgeschoß und im 1. Obergeschoß befinden sich die Räume der Damenabteilung, der Frisiersalon für Herren liegt im Untergeschoß.
Decken und Stützen wurden im ursprünglichen Zustand belassen, während die gesamte Einrichtung modern ist. Die neuen Lampen und Klimakanäle hängen mit deutlichem Abstand unter den alten Decken.

1. Entrance front. As in San Francisco, the salon interior is visible from the street through a glass front.
2. Reception area.
3. The ladies' salon on the upper floor.
4. The shampoo stations of the ladies' salon are reached by several steps.
5. Overall view of the ladies' salon.

1. Eingangsfront. Wie in San Francisco wurde auch hier das Innere des Salons von der Straße her durch eine Glasfront sichtbar gemacht.
2. Empfangsbereich.
3. Der Damensalon im Obergeschoß.
4. Die Schampunierplätze des Damensalons liegen einige Stufen erhöht.
5. Gesamtansicht des Damensalons.

De Berardinis hairdressing salon, Toronto
Architects: Francesco + Aldo Piccaluga Inc.

The unusual form of the De Berardinis hairdressing salon resulted from its construction around the ramp of the Eaton Centre parking garage.
A steep marble staircase leads from the pedestrian area to the interior which extends over three floors.
28 work tables equipped for ladies' and gentlemen's hairdressing (''unisex'') are arranged on the ramp side. Various partly-open rooms for washing, tinting etc. lie directly opposite, and a small cosmetic boutique a little lower.

Frisiersalon De Berardinis, Toronto
Architekten: Francesco + Aldo Piccaluga Inc.

Die ungewöhnliche Form des Frisiersalons De Berardinis ergab sich daraus, daß dieser um die Rampe der Parkgarage des Eaton Centre herum angelegt wurde.
Eine steile Marmortreppe führt aus dem Fußgängerbereich in das Innere, das sich über drei Ebenen erstreckt.
Auf der Rampenseite wurden 28 Arbeitstische angeordnet, die sowohl für Herren- als auch für Damenbedienung (»Unisex«) eingerichtet sind. Auf der gegenüberliegenden Seite befinden sich verschiedene halboffene Räume zum Waschen, Färben usw. sowie, etwas tiefer gelegen, eine kleine Kosmetik-Boutique.

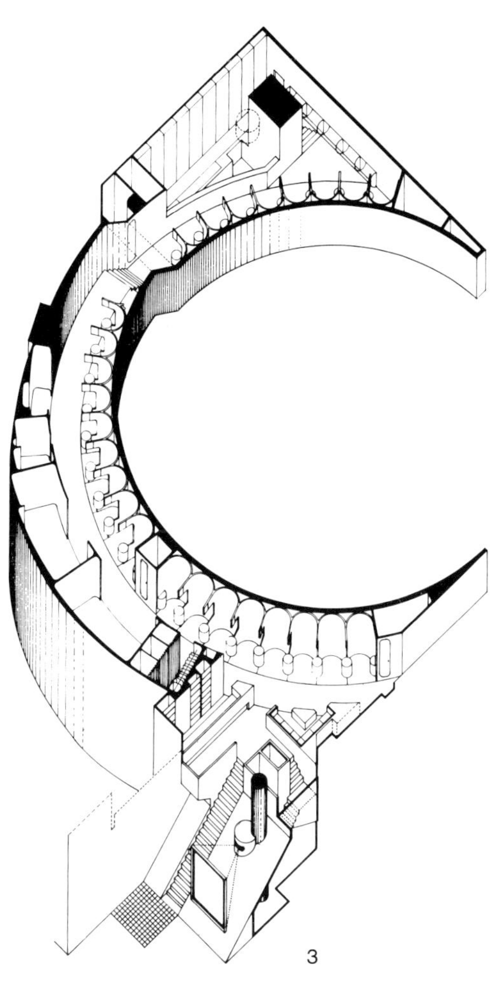

3

4

5

1. The stairs to the salon.
2. Reception area.
3. Axonometric view.
4. The work tables on the ramp side.
5. Shampoo stations.

1. Der Aufgang in den Salon.
2. Empfangsbereich.
3. Axonometrie.
4. Die Arbeitstische auf der Rampenseite.
5. Schampunierplätze.

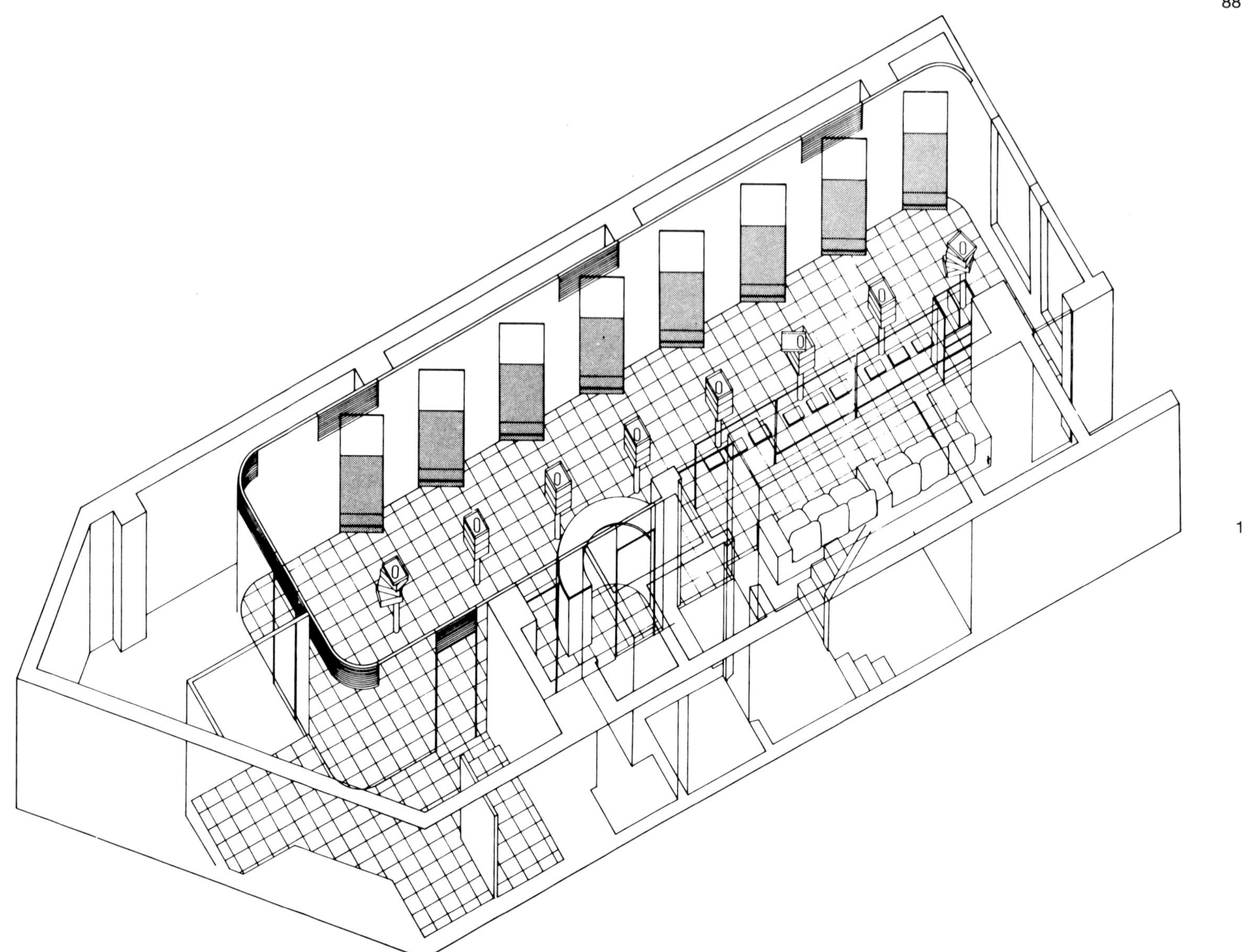

1

Koike beauty salon, Tokyo
Architect: Shiro Kuramata

The technical elegance of the Koike beauty shop hardly corresponds to the general concept of a shop of this type. Through the introduction of light-metal plates on walls and ceilings, glass, large-size mirrors and a floor covering of glazed white tiles, and impression of total transparency has been achieved, which detracts from the relatively austere room furnishings. The black upholstery on the customers' seats and benches forms a deliberate contrast to the light-coloured interior.

Schönheitssalon Koike, Tokio
Architekt: Shiro Kuramata

Der Schönheitssalon Koike entspricht in seiner technischen Eleganz kaum der Vorstellung üblicher Läden dieser Art. Durch die Verwendung von gebürsteten Leichtmetallplatten an Wänden und Decke, Glas, großformatigen Spiegeln und einem Bodenbelag aus weiß glasierten Fliesen wird in dem verhältnismäßig streng eingerichteten Raum der Eindruck von totaler Transparenz erzielt. Die Kundenstühle und die Sitzbänke mit schwarzer Polsterung stehen in bewußtem Kontrast zu dem hellen Raum.

1. Axonometric view.
2. View from the entrance into the customers' room. On the left the work stations, on the right the cash desk.
3–5. The work stations. The mirrors are suspended from the ceiling and hover over the floor. The necessary requisites are in depositories which are fixed on metal supports.

1. Axonometrie.
2. Blick vom Eingang in den Kundenraum. Links die Kundenplätze, rechts die Kasse.
3–5. Die Kundenplätze. Die Spiegel hängen von der Decke herab und schweben frei über dem Boden. Die notwendigen Requisiten befinden sich in Behältern, die an Säulen aus Metall befestigt sind.

2

4

5

3

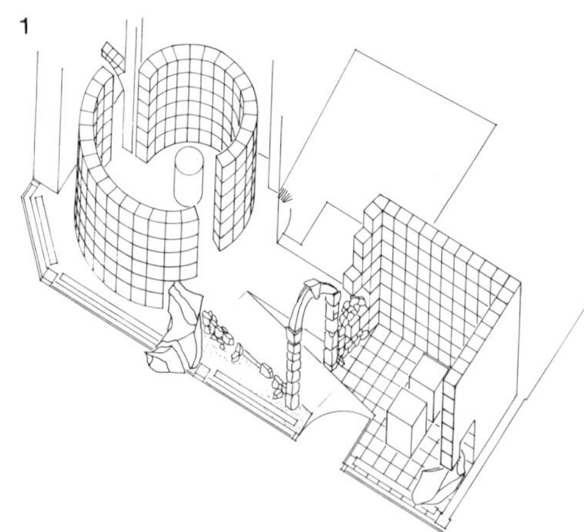

Pfeifenarchiv, Stuttgart

Architects: Arbeitsgemeinschaft für Architektur und Produktgestaltung (Peter Haas, Günter Hermann and Werner Schwarz)

The Pfeifenarchiv (which is a pipe shop) is situated in the Calwer Passage, which was built in the course of the redevelopment of Calwer Strasse as part of a new building complex planned by the architects Kammerer + Belz und Partner. The shop itself was to be accommodated in an area of 40 m^2, and no changes were to be made to the façade or to the room itself.

The pipes are selected and tested in a small rotunda which is modelled on Bramantes Tempietto in Rome. This "tempietto", whose walls consist of uniform-sized cuboid shelf elements, is the actual focal point of activity of the shop. Access to it is gained over a slightly sloping ramp which leads from a sandstone arch whose form and proportion are likewise derived from the Renaissance. The third area, which is adjacent to the entrance, is the "approach" where the cash desk is installed and where, in addition, lighters and other accessories as well as, in particular, cigars are sold. Cigars of the highest quality are displayed in a walk-in air-conditioned plexiglass cell which ensures constant temperature and air humidity. White-coated wall shelves in front of white walls form the background for these three areas.

Peifenarchiv, Stuttgart

Architekten: Arbeitsgemeinschaft für Architektur und Produktgestaltung (Peter Haas, Günter Hermann und Werner Schwarz)

Das Pfeifenarchiv liegt in der Calwer Passage, die im Zuge der Sanierung der Calwer Straße in einem von den Architekten Kammerer + Belz und Partner geplanten Neubaukomplex entstand. Für den Laden stand eine Fläche von 40 m^2 zur Verfügung; an der Fassade und am Raum selbst durfte nichts verändert werden.

Das Auswählen und Prüfen der Pfeifen erfolgt in einem kleinen Rundbau, der in Anlehnung an Bramantes Tempietto in Rom entstand. Dieser »Tempietto« – realisiert durch Wände aus gleich großen Regalkuben – bildet das eigentliche Zentrum des Ladengeschehens. Zu ihm führt eine leicht ansteigende Rampe, eröffnet durch einen in Form und Proportion ebenfalls der Renaissance entlehnten Torbogen aus Sandstein. Die dritte Zone ist das dem Eingang zugeordnete »Vorfeld«, in dem sich die Kasse befindet und wo außerdem Feuerzeuge und andere Accessoires sowie vor allem Zigarren verkauft werden. Die hochwertigsten Zigarren befinden sich in einer begehbaren Klimazelle aus Plexiglas, die eine gleichmäßige Temperatur und Luftfeuchtigkeit garantiert. Den Hintergrund für diese drei Zonen bilden weiß lackierte Regalwände vor weißen Wänden.

1. Axonometric view.
2. The entrance front seen from the other side of
the gallery.
3. Plan. Key: 1 entrance, 2 cigars, 3 lighters,
4 seats, 5 tobacco, 6 pipes, 7 display.
4. View from the ''tempietto'' through the sandstone arch towards the entrance area.

1. Axonometrie.
2. Die Eingangsfront über die Passage hinweg
gesehen.
3. Grundriß. Legende: 1 Eingang, 2 Zigarren,
3 Feuerzeuge, 4 Sitzplätze, 5 Tabak, 6 Pfeifen,
7 Auslage.
4. Blick vom »Tempietto« durch den Sandstein-
bogen in Richtung auf den Eingangsbereich.

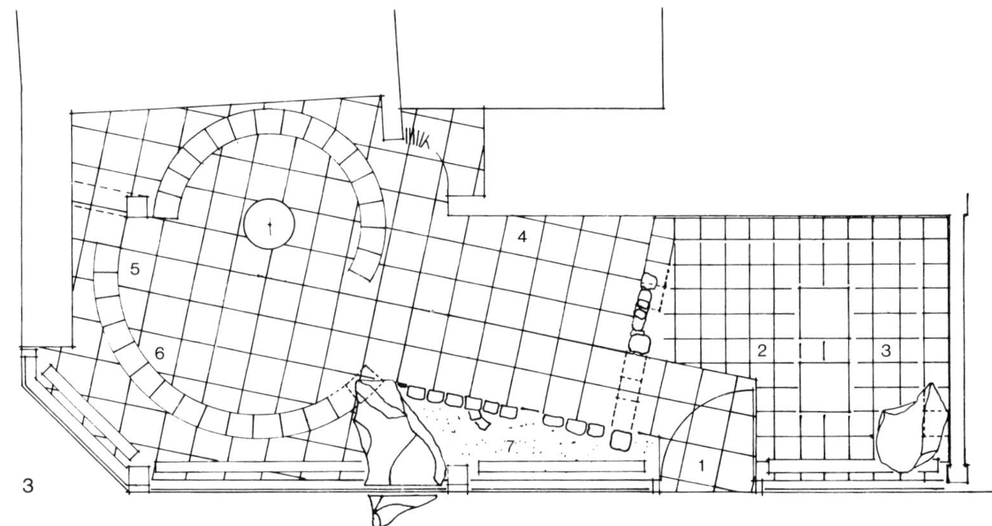

3

4

PFEIFENARCHIV
STUTTGART
CALWERPASSAGE

GRUNDELEMENTE REGALSYSTEM

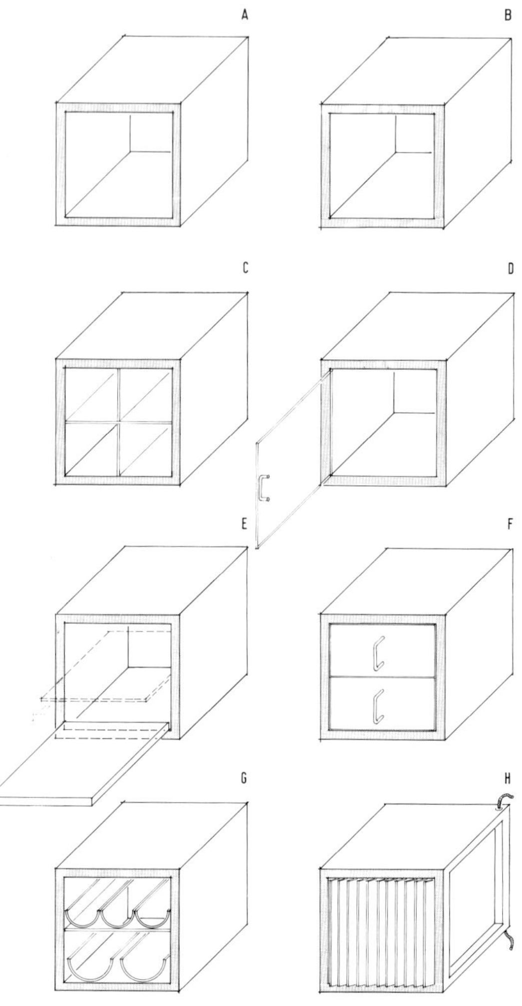

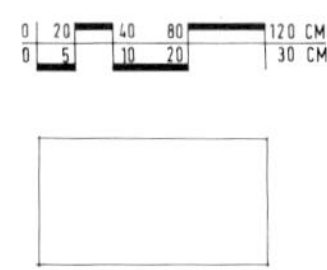

A GRUNDELEMENT
WEISS LACKIERT
SICHTBARE KANTEN SCHWARZ
ZWEISEITIG OFFEN
WAHLWEISE AUSSTATTUNG MIT
- LEDER
- SPIEGELFLÄCHEN

B GRUNDELEMENT MIT FACHBODEN
AUSFÜHRUNG IN
- GLASBODEN
- SPIEGELFLÄCHE
- LEDERBÖDEN

C GRUNDELEMENT MIT FACHKREUZ
AUSFÜHRUNG IN
- PLEXIGLAS
- LEDERFLÄCHEN

D GRUNDELEMENT MIT RÜCKWAND
UND VORDERSEITIGER GLASTÜRE

E GRUNDELEMENT MIT RÜCKWAND
UND VORDERSEITIGER GESCHLOSSENER
TÜRE
MIT FACHBODEN

F GRUNDELEMENT MIT RÜCKWAND
UND VORDERSEITIG 2 SCHUBLADEN
GESCHLOSSEN

G GRUNDELEMENT MIT TABAKDOSEN-
EINSÄTZEN
PLEXIGLASBÖDEN MIT
AUFGESETZTEN , HALBRUNDEN
SCHALEN
⌀ 90 , ⌀ 100 , ⌀ 120

H GRUNDELEMENT ALS BELEUCHTUNGS-
EINHEIT
5 - SEITIG OFFEN
2 SEITEN UND BODEN
MIT EINGELEGTEM MILCHGLAS
VOR-UND RÜCKSEITE
MIT EINGESETZTEN MILCHGLAS-
LAMELLEN
BESTÜCKUNG MIT QUECKSILBER-
DAMPFLAMPE 50 WATT

MONTAGEEINHEIT REGALSYSTEM

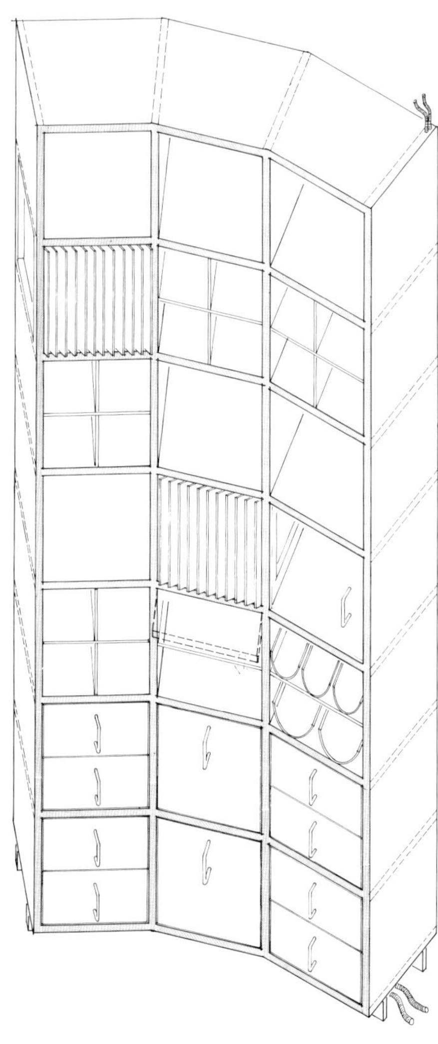

ADDITION DER ELEMENTE

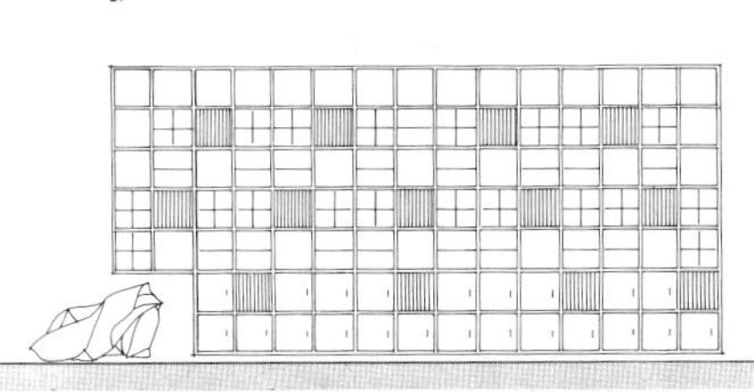

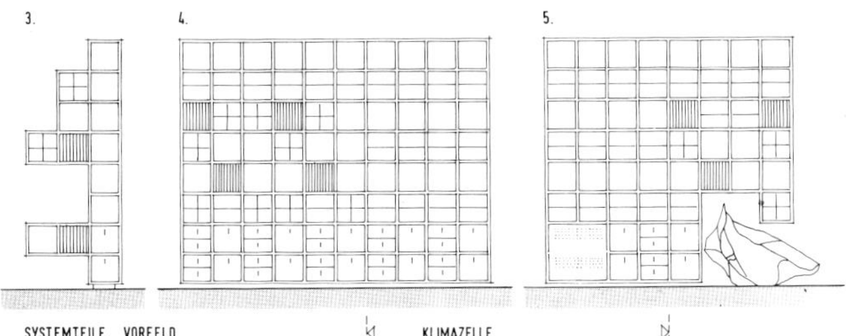

5. Detail of the shelf cubes (basic elements, fitting unit, combination of the elements). Key: A basic element, B basic element with horizontal partition, C basic element with cross-shaped partition, D basic element with back wall and glass front door, E basic element with back wall and closed front door, F basic element with back wall and two drawers, G basic element with insets for tobacco boxes, H basic element as lighting unit, 1,2 semicircles for the "tempietto", 3,4,5 system parts for the "approach" (with air-conditioned cell).
6. View into the "tempietto".
7. "Approach".

5. Detail der Regalkuben (Grundelemente, Montageeinheit, Addition der Elemente). Legende: A Grundelement, B Grundelement mit Fachboden, C Grundelement mit Fachkreuz, D Grundelement mit Rückwand und vorderseitiger Glastür, E Grundelement mit Rückwand und vorderseitiger geschlossener Tür, F Grundelement mit Rückwand und zwei Schubladen, G Grundelement mit Tabakdoseneinsätzen, H Grundelement als Beleuchtungseinheit, 1,2 Halbrunde für den »Tempietto«, 3,4,5 Systemteile für das »Vorfeld« (mit Klimazelle).
6. Blick in den »Tempietto«.
7. »Vorfeld«.

6

7

2

Max Pock university bookshop, Graz

Architects: Team A Graz (Franz Cziharz, Dietrich Ecker, Herbert Missoni and Jörg Wallmüller); assistant: Karin Wallmüller

The Max Pock university bookshop was established as a book and music shop on the ground floor of the newly built Graz town hall in 1891. When converting the building, the architects had to pay particular attention to preserving the structure of the façade and the building. The basis for their deliberations was the desire to combine modern presentation, sales and operating methods with the traditional atmosphere of the old bookshop.
The architectural design is based on the structural elements present in the building structure – wall masses, arch openings, transverse arches and vaults. Due to the open-front character of the shop, the changing daylight effects and the hustle and bustle on the square in front of the town hall are integrated into the experience of the interior.
The texture of the fittings emphasizes the structural division of the rooms. The organized character and the dark oak of the individual elements – shelves, staircase, gallery parapets, wall coverings, waffle ceilings – form a striking contrast to the colourful variety of books.

Universitätsbuchhandlung Max Pock, Graz

Architekten: Team A Graz (Franz Cziharz, Dietrich Ecker, Herbert Missoni und Jörg Wallmüller); Mitarbeiterin: Karin Wallmüller

Die Universitätsbuchhandlung Max Pock wurde 1891 als Buch- und Musikalienhandlung im Erdgeschoß des damals neu erbauten Grazer Rathauses eingerichtet. Beim Umbau hatten die Architekten besonders auf die Bewahrung der Fassaden- und Gebäudestruktur zu achten. Ausgangspunkt ihrer Überlegungen war der Wunsch, neuzeitliche Präsentations-, Verkaufs- und Betriebsmethoden im Buchhandel mit der traditionellen Atmosphäre des alten Buchladens zu verbinden.
Das architektonische Konzept der Neugestaltung baut auf den in der baulichen Hülle vorgefundenen Strukturelementen – Mauermassen, Bogenöffnungen, Gurtbögen, Gewölbe – auf. Durch eine weitgehende Öffnung der Schaufenster wurde die Wirkung des wechselnden Tageslichts und das geschäftige Treiben auf dem Platz vor dem Rathaus in das Erlebnis des Innenraums einbezogen.
Die Struktur der Einrichtung soll die bauliche Gliederung des Raums betonen. Die einzelnen Elemente – Regale, Treppe, Galeriebrüstungen, Wandverkleidungen, Kassettendecken – wirken durch die strenge Unterteilung und die dunkle Farbe des Eichenholzes als Ordnungsfaktor gegenüber der bunten Vielfalt der Bücher.

3
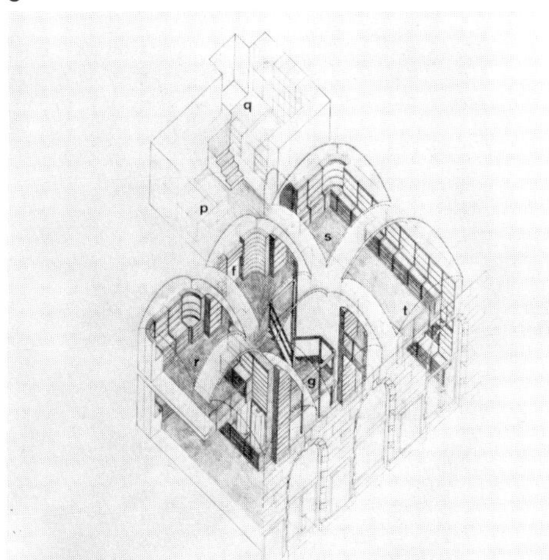
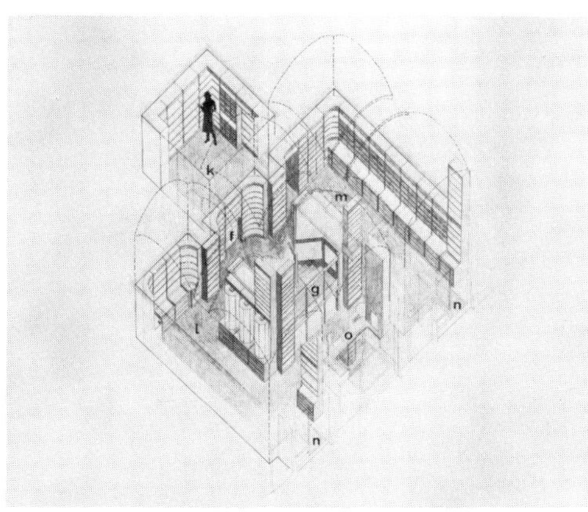
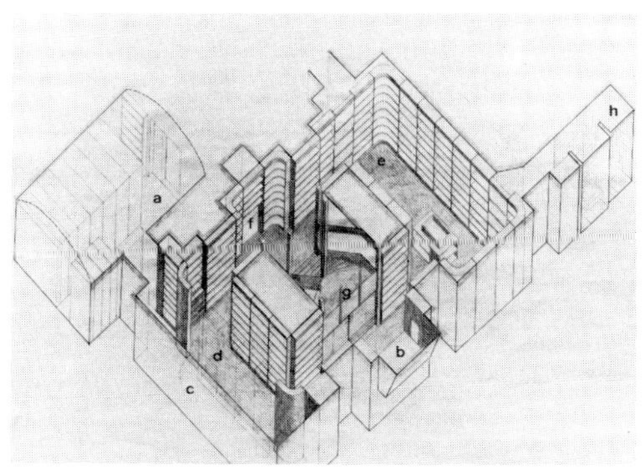

4

1. In the course of conversion the façade of the building was preserved as far as possible.
2. View from the gallery floor towards the town-hall square.
3. Axonometric views (basement, ground floor, gallery floor). Key: a store, b working table with lift for books, c packing room, d educational books, e books for children and juveniles, f lift for small goods, g stairs, h lavatory and WC, k office, l publications of topical interest, tourism, belles-lettres, pocket-books, m music department, n entrances, o cash desk, p office and mailing, q staff rooms, r art books, s sciences, t working and sitting area.
4. Ground floor with suspended gallery floor.

1. Beim Umbau wurde die Fassade des Gebäudes weitestgehend bewahrt.
2. Blick vom Galeriegeschoß auf den Rathausplatz.
3. Axonometrien (Untergeschoß, Erdgeschoß, Galeriegeschoß). Legende: a Lager, b Arbeitstisch mit Bücheraufzug, c Packraum, d Schulbücher, e Kinder- und Jugenbücher, f Kleinlastenaufzug, g Treppe, h Waschraum und WC, k Büro, l Aktuelles, Tourismus, Belletristik, Taschenbücher, m Musikabteilung, n Eingänge, o Kasse, p Büro und Versand, q Personalräume, r Kunstbücher, s Wissenschaften, t Arbeits- und Sitzbereich.
4. Erdgeschoß mit eingehängtem Galeriegeschoß.

1

Franz Deuticke publishing house, Vienna
Architects: Karl and Eva Mang

2

Since the house in which the bookshop is accommodated is situated in the Ringstrasse area, which is an urban preservation area, the renovation of its exterior was carried out with the special attention paid to the preservation of historic buildings. The interior, on the other hand, was completely reorganized and adapted to present-day requirements.
Retail books and antiquarian books are displayed to advantage (spatially and functionally) in one large room. Greater use could be made of this very high room, which was built around the turn of the century, by adding a gallery which can be easily reached by two staircases. Dark, neutral wood (wengé) accentuates the colourful variety of books on display.

Verlagsbuchhandlung Franz Deuticke, Wien
Architekten: Karl und Eva Mang

Da das Haus, in dem die Buchhandlung untergebracht ist, in der unter Bereichsschutz stehenden Ringstraßenzone liegt, wurde das Äußere unter dem Gesichtspunkt der Denkmalpflege behandelt. Im Gegensatz dazu erfuhr der Innenraum eine völlige Neugestaltung im Sinn unserer Zeit.
Sortiment und Antiquariat ließen sich sowohl räumlich als auch von der Funktion her gut in dem vorhandenen Großraum unterbringen. Der hohe Raum, um die Jahrhundertwende gebaut, konnte durch den Einbau einer Galerie, die über zwei bequeme Treppen erreichbar ist, in seiner Nutzung intensiviert werden. Dunkles, neutrales Holz (Wenge) unterstreicht die Farbigkeit und Vielfalt der ausgestellten Bücher.

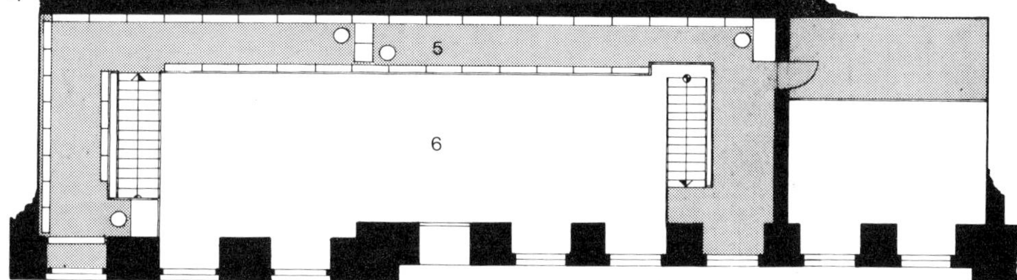

3

1. Street front.
2. View through the entrance into the salesroom.
3. Salesroom. On the left the street side, on the right the gallery.
4. Plans (ground floor, gallery floor). Key:
1 office, 2 antiquarian books, 3 retail book-trade, 4 office and cloakroom, 5 gallery, 6 void, 7 publishing department.

1. Straßenfront.
2. Blick durch den Eingang in den Verkaufsraum.
3. Verkaufsraum. Links die Straßenseite, rechts die Galerie.
4. Grundrisse (Erdgeschoß, Galeriegeschoß). Legende: 1 Büro, 2 Antiquariat, 3 Sortiment, 4 Büro und Garderobe, 5 Galerie, 6 Luftraum, 7 Verlag.

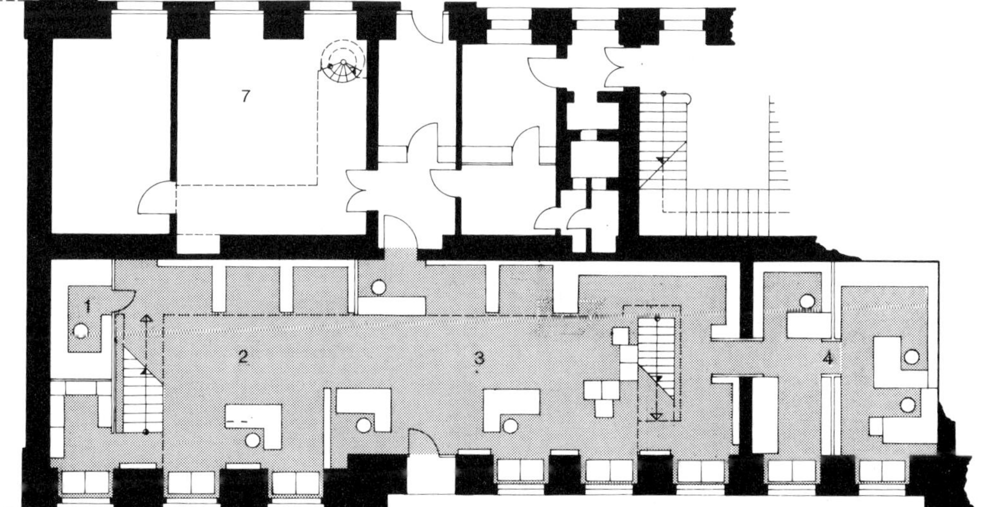

2

1

Pocket-book department of the Morawa & Co. bookshop, Vienna
Architects: Karl and Eva Mang
Graphic design: Atelier Heinz Ehrenfels

The newly opened pocket-book department of the Morawa bookshop in Vienna's Wollzeile is separated from the main shop solely by a courtyard entrance.
The design of the exterior is based on the covered arcade and the façade of the main shop which blends with the historical surroundings; the external appearance of the main shop was decided upon when it was designed over 15 years ago, in agreement with the office for the preservation of historical monuments.
The three room-dividing elements – the floor (plastic finish), the walls (painted black to provide a neutral background) and the suspended prefabricated ceiling which serves as a light support and module for the interior construction – form a fixed system which allows complete variability in the arrangement of the shop-window construction and the furnishings.

Taschenbuchabteilung der Buchhandlung Morawa & Co., Wien
Architekten: Karl und Eva Mang
Graphische Gestaltung: Atelier Heinz Ehrenfels

Die neu eingerichtete Taschenbuchabteilung der Buchhandlung Morawa in der Wiener Wollzeile ist lediglich durch eine Hofeinfahrt vom Hauptgeschäft getrennt.
Ausgangspunkte für die Außenform waren die gedeckte Passage und die sich dem historischen Bestand unterordnende Front des Hauptgeschäfts, dessen äußere Erscheinung bei seinem Entwurf vor über 15 Jahren mit dem Denkmalamt abgesprochen worden war.
Die drei den Raum begrenzenden Elemente – der Fußboden (Kunststoffbelag), die Wände (schwarz gestrichen, um einen neutralen Hintergrund abzugeben) und die als Lichtträger und Modul für die Innenkonstruktion dienende abgehängte Montagedecke bilden ein Festsystem, in das die Schaufensterkonstruktion und die Möblierung völlig variabel eingeordnet werden können.

1, 2. Entrance area.
3. Plans (on the left first stage, on the right extension).
4. Salesroom. To allow for changes in the sales programme at short notice, a variable system based on a simple steel construction was developed both for the shop-window construction as well as for the whole interior.

1, 2. Eingangszone.
3. Grundrisse (links 1. Ausbaustufe, rechts Erweiterung).
4. Verkaufsraum. Um das Verkaufsprogramm kurzfristig ändern zu können, wurde sowohl für die Schaufensterkonstruktion als auch für den gesamten Innenraum ein variables System auf der Basis einer einfachen Stahlkonstruktion entwickelt.

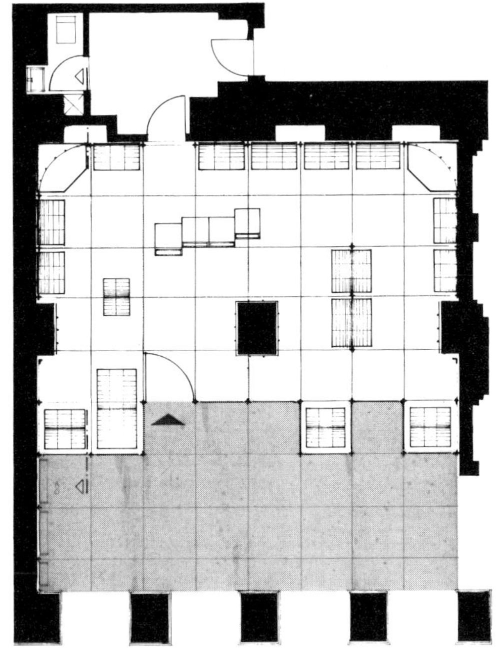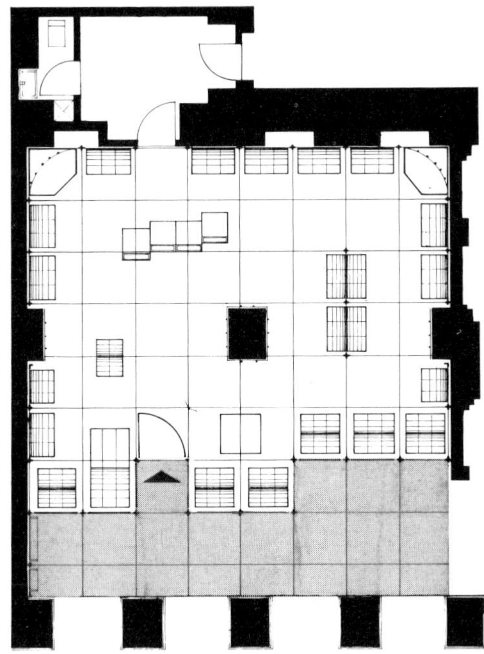

3

4

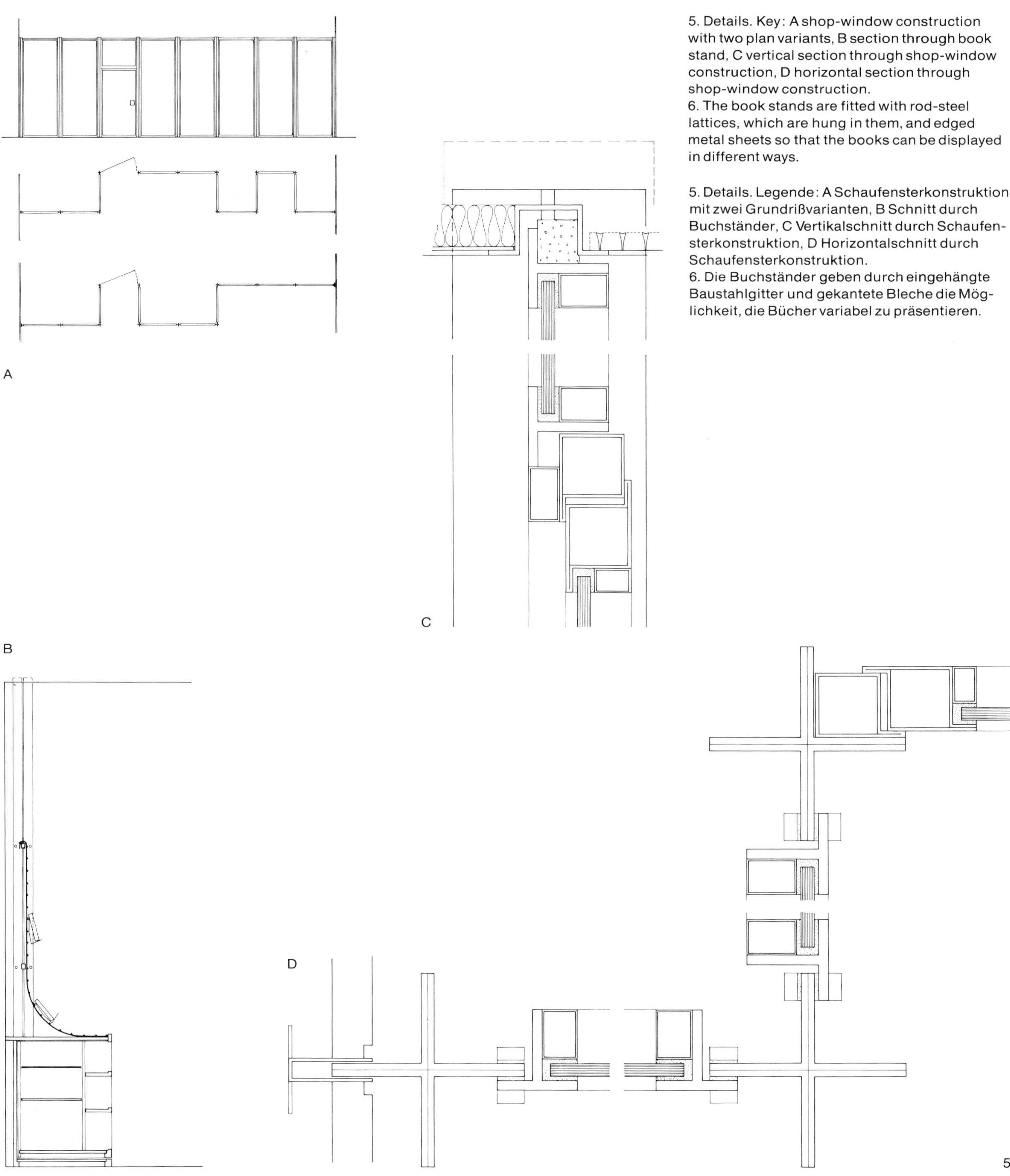

5. Details. Key: A shop-window construction with two plan variants, B section through book stand, C vertical section through shop-window construction, D horizontal section through shop-window construction.
6. The book stands are fitted with rod-steel lattices, which are hung in them, and edged metal sheets so that the books can be displayed in different ways.

5. Details. Legende: A Schaufensterkonstruktion mit zwei Grundrißvarianten, B Schnitt durch Buchständer, C Vertikalschnitt durch Schaufensterkonstruktion, D Horizontalschnitt durch Schaufensterkonstruktion.
6. Die Buchständer geben durch eingehängte Baustahlgitter und gekantete Bleche die Möglichkeit, die Bücher variabel zu präsentieren.

etristik
Sachbücher
Praktische
Reihen
Kriminalro

Peter Eaton Ltd. bookshop, London
Architects: Rick Mather Architects

The Peter Eaton bookshop contains a department for antiquarian books on the ground floor, and a mail-order department for libraries in the basement, as well as offices on both floors. The owner's two-storey appartment is above. The whole complex resulted from the extension of an old building of which the two upper storeys with the apartment are the only remaining parts.

To get a continuous space below it, the old building was underpinned with a steel construction. By superimposing the new and old buildings, interconnected levels were created which divide the rooms and at the same time heighten their visual attraction. Access to the shop is clearly defined: one entrance leads directly to the department for antiquarian books, a second entrance adjacent to it leads down a staircase to the mail-order department in the basement, which is also connected to the ground-floor rooms by an internal staircase.

In order to allow as much daylight as possible to enter the new rooms, a roof-light was put in over the ground floor and an opening at the same point in the ceiling above the basement.

The architectural concept of a bookshop which opens on to the street is underlined in a variety of delightful ways not only by the all-glass front but also by the different levels, clever lighting, the use of plants and by reflecting parapet surfaces.

Buchhandlung Peter Eaton Ltd., London
Architekten: Rick Mather Architects

Die Buchhandlung Peter Eaton Ltd. gliedert sich in ein Antiquariat im Erdgeschoß, einen Bücherversand für Bibliotheken im Untergeschoß sowie Büros auf beiden Ebenen. Darüber liegt die zweigeschossige Wohnung des Eigentümers. Das Ganze ist das Ergebnis einer wesentlichen Erweiterung eines älteren Gebäudes, von dem nur die beiden Obergeschosse mit der Wohnung erhalten blieben.

Der Altbau wurde mit einer Stahlkonstruktion unterfangen, um darunter nicht auf durchlaufende Flächen verzichten zu müssen. Das Übereinander von Neu- und Altbau nutzte man für die Anlage ineinander verschachtelter Ebenen, die die Räume gliedern und zugleich deren visuelle Attraktivität erhöhen. Die Erschließung ist übersichtlich: Ein Zugang führt direkt in das Antiquariat, daneben führt ein zweiter über eine Treppe zu dem Buchversand im Untergeschoß, das mit den Erdgeschoßräumen zusätzlich durch eine interne Treppe verbunden ist.

Um in den neuen Räumen möglichst viel Tageslicht zu erhalten, wurde über dem Erdgeschoß ein Oberlicht und in der Decke über dem Untergeschoß an der gleichen Stelle ein Deckendurchbruch angeordnet.

Die architektonische Konzeption einer zur Straße offenen Buchhandlung wird nicht nur durch die vollständige Verglasung der Front, sondern auch durch die verschiedenen Ebenen, eine geschickte Lichtführung, Pflanzen sowie durch spiegelnde Brüstungen vielfältig und reizvoll unterstrichen.

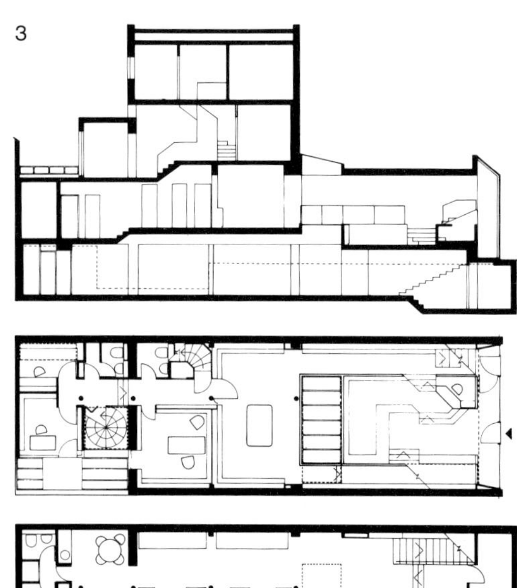

1

2

3

1. View from the department for antiquarian books towards the street.
2. Entrance front. The entrance on the left leads directly to the department for antiquarian books, the entrance on the right leads down a staircase to the mail-order department in the basement.
3. Plans (basement, ground floor) and section.
4, 5. The department for antiquarian books on the ground floor.

1. Blick vom Antiquariat auf die Straße.
2. Eingangsfront. Der linke Zugang führt direkt in das Antiquariat, der rechte Zugang über eine Treppe zum Bücherversand im Untergeschoß.
3. Grundrisse (Untergeschoß, Erdgeschoß) und Schnitt.
4, 5. Das Antiquariat im Erdgeschoß.

5 4

Academic Bookshop, Helsinki
Architect: Alvar Aalto

Situated in the centre of Helsinki, the Academic Bookshop is housed on the lower floors of a commercial building on the corner of Keskuskatu and Esplanadi, which was also planned by Alvar Aalto.

There are entrances from both streets, which are accentuated by indentations in the façade front. A stationer's shop, connected to the bookshop, is accommodated in the corner area between the two entrances.

The bookshop itself is a hall which extends up three floors and includes two galleries, the first of which is reached by an escalator, since it forms a continuation of the sales area on the ground floor. Three large roof-lights, the shapes of which resemble that of rock crystals, equipped with additional lighting fixtures, let daylight into the hall.

Eye-level bookshelves are located for the most part in the lower areas, while in the central area book-tables are arranged with rack-shelves directly above, allowing the front of a large number of books to be seen on the self-service principle.

Akademische Buchhandlung, Helsinki
Architekt: Alvar Aalto

Die Akademische Buchhandlung, im Zentrum Helsinkis gelegen, befindet sich in den unteren Geschossen eines ebenfalls von Alvar Aalto geplanten Geschäftshauses an der Ecke Keskuskatu und Esplanadi.

Es gibt von beiden Straßen aus Zugänge, die durch Einbuchtungen in der Fassadenfront betont sind. Die Eckzone zwischen den beiden Zugängen beherbergt eine mit der Buchhandlung verbundene Papeterie.

Die Buchhandlung selbst ist eine über drei Stockwerke gehende Halle mit zwei Galerien, von denen die erste über eine Rolltreppe erschlossen wird, da sie wie das Erdgeschoß dem Verkauf dient. Die Halle erhält Tageslicht durch drei große, in der Form an Bergkristalle erinnernde Oberlichter mit zusätzlich eingebauten Beleuchtungskörpern.

In den niedrigen Zonen befinden sich größtenteils Bücherregale in Mannshöhe, während in der zentralen Zone Büchertische mit darüber angeordneten Tablaren aufgestellt sind, die es ermöglichen, viele Bücher in Frontalansicht zu zeigen, wie es das Selbstbedienungsprinzip verlangt.

3

1. The bookshop is housed in a commercial building, which was also planned by Alvar Aalto.
2. View from the first gallery into the sales hall. Three large roof-lights, equipped with additional lighting fixtures, let daylight into the hall.
3. Sales hall.
4. Plan (ground floor) and section.

1. Die Buchhandlung befindet sich in einem ebenfalls von Alvar Aalto geplanten Geschäftshaus.
2. Blick von der ersten Galerie in die Verkaufshalle. Die Halle erhält Tageslicht durch drei große Oberlichter mit zusätzlich eingebauten Beleuchtungskörpern.
3. Verkaufshalle.
4. Grundriß (Erdgeschoß) und Schnitt.

4

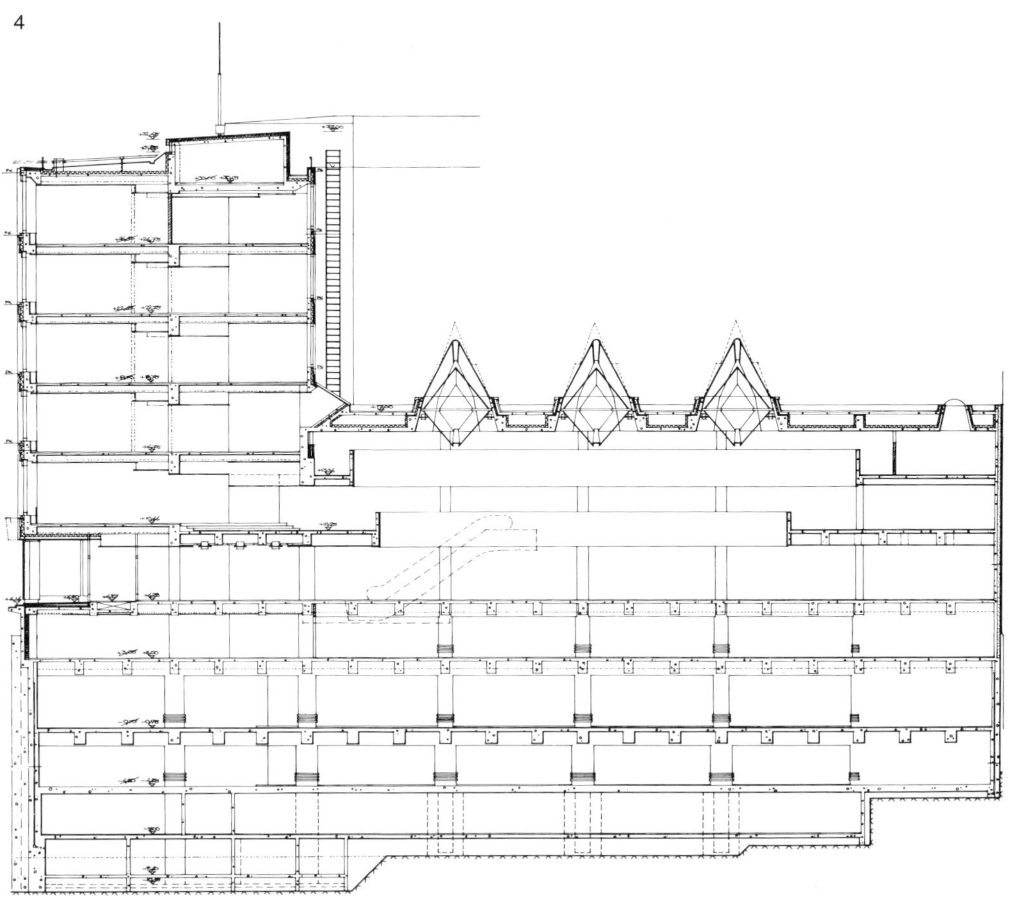

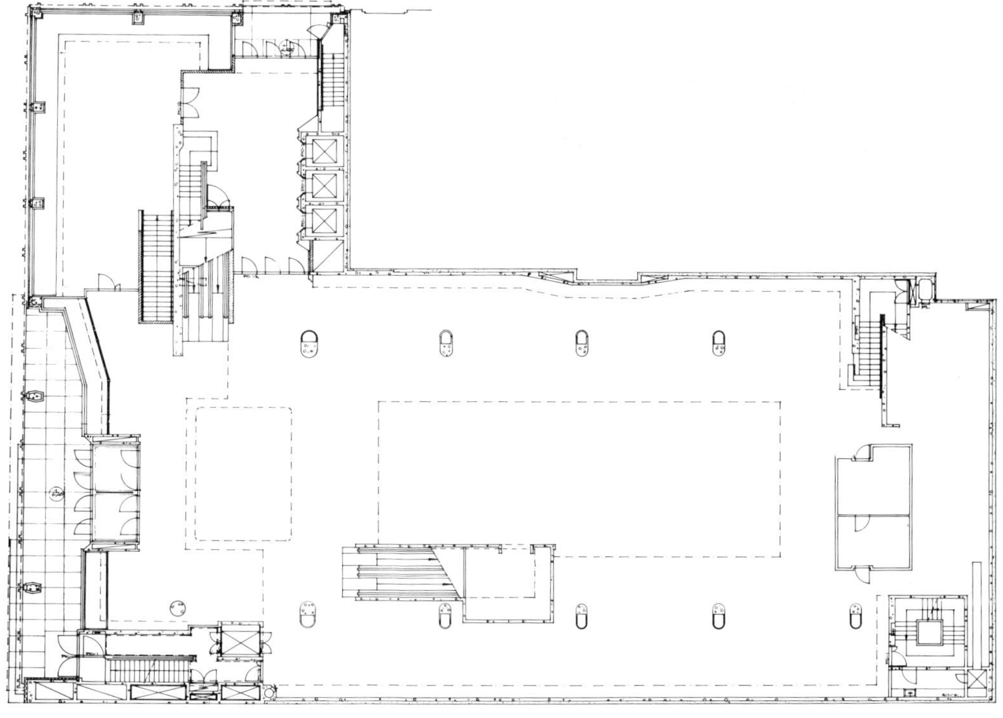

1

Morgental Apotheke, Zurich
Architects: Robert Haussmann and Trix Haussmann-Högl

The Morgental Apotheke is in a residential area that has houses dating back to the thirties. The main problem presented by renovation was to find a solution which, despite the extremely confined space, would satisfy functional as well as formal requirements.
The external appearance of the pharmacy is characterized by its façade of spray-galvanized and pre-patinated iron sheets with preset chrome-plated steel pipes and rounded windows in lead glazing. This stands out very distinctly from its surroundings. The interior presents lively contrasts between black rubber floor tiles, wooden cupboards painted white, white plexiglass lamps and large mirrored surfaces.

Morgental Apotheke, Zürich
Architekten: Robert Haussmann und Trix Haussmann-Högl

Die Morgental Apotheke liegt in einem Wohngebiet mit Häusern aus den dreißiger Jahren. Das Hauptproblem bei ihrer Erneuerung bestand darin, eine Lösung zu finden, die trotz äußerst beengter Raumverhältnisse sowohl funktional als auch gestalterisch befriedigt. Das äußere Erscheinungsbild der Apotheke wird geprägt durch die sich stark von ihrer Umgebung abhebende Fassade aus spritzverzinkten und patinierten Eisenplatten mit davorgesetzten Rohren aus verchromtem Stahl und ausgerundeten Fenstern in Bleiverglasung. Das Innere lebt vom Kontrast zwischen schwarzen Bodenplatten aus Gummi, weiß lackierten Holzschränken, weißen Plexiglaslampen und großen Spiegelflächen.

1. The façade stands out very distinctly from its surroundings.
2. Plan and elevation.
3. View from outside towards the entrance.
4, 5. The interior presents a lively contrast between black rubber floor tiles, wooden cupboards painted white, white plexiglass lamps and large mirrored surfaces.

1. Die Außenfront setzt sich stark von ihrer Umgebung ab.
2. Grundriß und Ansicht.
3. Blick von außen auf den Eingang.
4, 5. Das Innere der Apotheke lebt vom Kontrast zwischen schwarzen Bodenplatten aus Gummi, weiß lackierten Holzschränken, weißen Plexiglaslampen und großen Spiegelflächen.

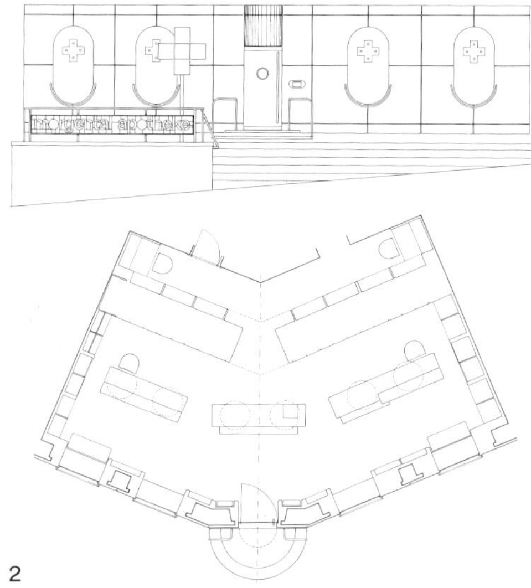

2

4

3

5

1. The old Kron-Apotheke in 1975 shortly before its demolition.
2. The new pharmacy fits well into its surroundings.

1. Die alte Kron-Apotheke im Jahr 1975 kurz vor dem Abbruch.
2. Die neue Apotheke paßt sich gut in ihre Umgebung ein.

2

Kron-Apotheke, Stuttgart-Bad Cannstatt

Architect: Werner Luz; assistants: Uwe Hübenbecker and Axel Asseburg

The Kron-Apotheke is located in the Marktstrasse in the midst of the centre of Bad Cannstatt, one of the few districts of Stuttgart which has retained part of its mediaeval character. Since the old shop building was badly in need of repair and, moreover, could not have fulfilled the present-day requirements of a pharmacy, it was pulled down in spite of its historical value.

A skeleton system of reinforced concrete was chosen for the new building. Its dimensions were proportioned according to use, with the pharmacy on the ground floor, five doctor consulting rooms on the three floors above and two apartments in the attic, and also according to the outline form of the building, which is adapted to its surroundings. The structure system extends to the façade and, together with the "dimensional supports" for partition walls and windows, constitutes the dominating element of design.

Kron-Apotheke, Stuttgart-Bad Cannstatt

Architekt: Werner Luz; Mitarbeiter: Uwe Hübenbecker und Axel Asseburg

Die Kron-Apotheke liegt an der Markstraße, mitten im Kern von Bad Cannstatt, der zu den wenigen Gebieten Stuttgarts mit noch mittelalterlichem Gepräge gehört. Da das alte Apothekengebäude baulich in einem sehr schlechten Zustand war und obendrein die Erfüllung heutiger Forderungen an eine Apotheke sehr erschwert hätte, wurde es trotz seiner historischen Wertschätzung abgerissen.

Für den Neubau wurde ein Stahlbetonskelettsystem gewählt, das in seinen Abmessungen auf die Nutzung – im Erdgeschoß die Apotheke, in den drei Geschossen darüber fünf Arztpraxen und im Dachgeschoß zwei Wohnungen – und die an die Umgebung angepaßte Umrißform des Gebäudes abgestimmt wurde. Das Tragsystem wurde bis an die Außenfront vorgezogen und bildet zusammen mit den zur Aufnahme von Trennwänden und Fenstern nötigen »Maßstützen« das bestimmende Gestaltungselement.

1

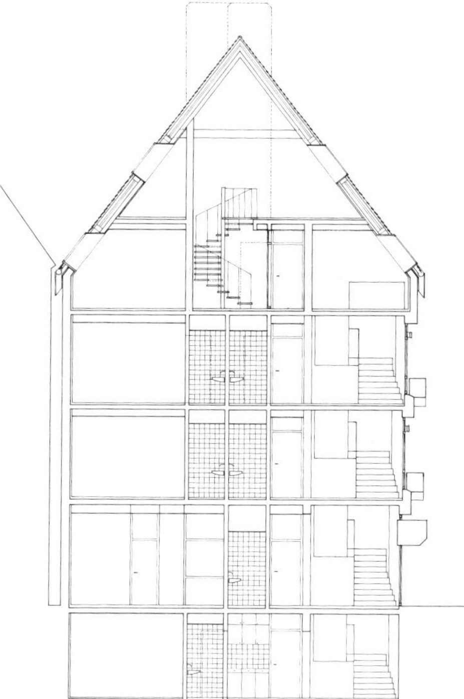

4

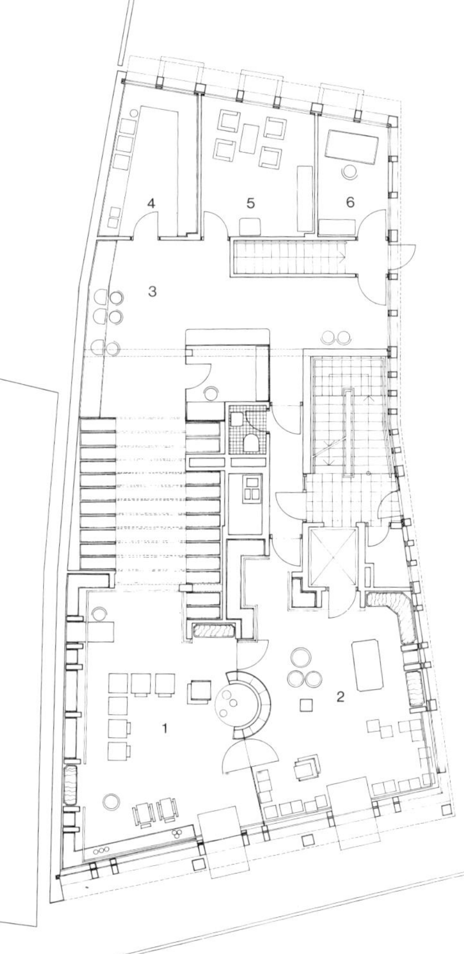

3

5

3. Plan (ground floor) and section. Key: 1 pharmacy, 2 druggery, 3 small store, 4 laboratory, 5 staff room, 6 office.

4. Entrance front. The structural system extends to the façade and, together with the "dimensional supports" for partition walls and windows, constitutes the dominating element of design.

5. The salesroom of the pharmacy.

3. Grundriß (Erdgeschoß) und Schnitt. Legende: 1 Apotheke, 2 Drogerie, 3 Handlager, 4 Labor, 5 Personal, 6 Büro.

4. Eingangsfront. Das Tragsystem wurde bis an die Außenfront vorgezogen und bildet zusammen mit den zur Aufnahme von Trennwänden und Fenstern nötigen »Maßstützen« das bestimmende Gestaltungselement.

5. Der Verkaufsraum der Apotheke.

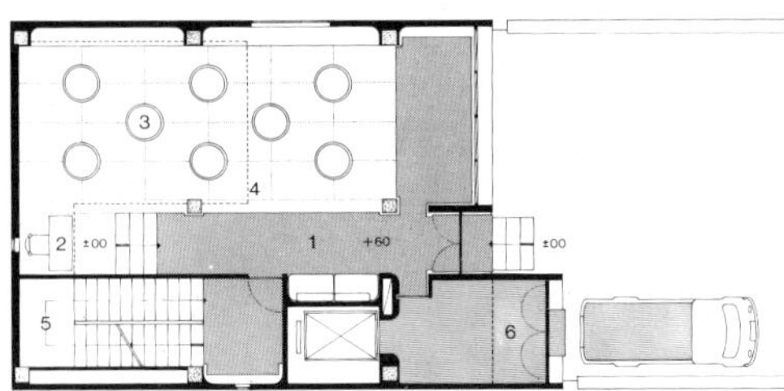

1

2

Display room for paints near Beirut
Architects: Francesco + Aldo Piccaluga Inc.

The small display room of the DEFA company, paint manufacturers, is in a building on the motorway outside the town.
The very individual shape of the building as well as the distinctive lettering, which is orientated to both driving directions, is designed to attract the attention of passing motorists. The display room is located on the ground floor. Colour pigments and materials are displayed in eight cylindrical showcases in a slightly recessed room opposite the entrance area.

Ausstellungsraum für Farben bei Beirut
Architekten: Francesco + Aldo Piccaluga Inc.

Der kleine Ausstellungsraum der Firma DEFA, eines Unternehmens der Farbenbranche, befindet sich in einem Gebäude an der Autobahn etwas außerhalb der Stadt.
Die einprägsame Form des Baus soll die Aufmerksamkeit der vorüberfahrenden Autofahrer ebenso erregen wie die nach beiden Fahrtrichtungen orientierten, weithin sichtbaren Schriftzüge. Der Ausstellungsraum liegt im Erdgeschoß. In dem gegenüber dem Eingangsbereich etwas abgesetzten Raum werden in acht zylindrischen Vitrinen Farbpigmente und Materialien zur Schau gestellt.

1. View across the street towards the building.
2. Plan. Key: 1 raised entrance area, 2 information, 3 cylindrical showcases, 4 line of mezzanine, 5 stairs to basement and mezzanine, 6 loading dock.
3. Overall view of the display room towards the street.
4. Showcase.
5. View from the raised entrance area towards the information desk.

1. Blick über die Straße hinweg auf das Gebäude.
2. Grundriß. Legende: 1 angehobener Eingangsbereich, 2 Information, 3 zylindrische Vitrinen, 4 Umriß des Zwischengeschosses, 5 Treppe zum Unter- und zum Zwischengeschoß, 6 Laderampe.
3. Gesamtansicht des Ausstellungsraums in Richtung Straße.
4. Ausstellungsvitrine.
5. Blick vom angehobenen Eingangsbereich in Richtung Informationsplatz.

1. Entrance front.
2. Plan and section.
3. View into the right-hand part of the salesroom.
On the gallery the manager's work-table, underneath, books and other small goods.

1. Eingangsfront.
2. Grundriß und Schnitt.
3. Blick in den rechten Teil des Verkaufsraumes.
Auf der Galerie der Arbeitsplatz der Geschäftsführung, darunter Bücher und andere kleinere Verkaufsartikel.

1

Feldhaus Kind + Kindergarten toy shop, Cologne
Architects: Koerber + Hager

Feldhaus Kind + Kindergarten, which specializes in hand-made and educational toys as well as kindergarten requisites, is accommodated in one of the rented rooms of the St. Columba Franciscan monastery. Additional store and display rooms for large kindergarten equipment are to be found in the basement rooms under the court.
The entrance leads directly to the centre of the room where the cash desk and wrapping counter are arranged. The manager's desk and consultation tables are situated on the recessed gallery in the right half of the room. Books and other smaller sales articles are displayed below in an extremely low section of the shop. The left section of the shop is of normal room height and offers seating accommodation.
The goods are displayed in a simple unit construction system: each wall has been fitted with planks arranged one above the other and spaced according to the thickness of the shelves. The shelves are inserted into the slots; their rear end has been shaped in such a way that they are held in position through the weight of the goods and do not require additional fixtures.

Spielwarengeschäft Feldhaus Kind + Kindergarten, Köln
Architekten: Koerber + Hager

Feldhaus Kind + Kindergarten, ein Spezialgeschäft für kunstgewerbliches und pädagogisches Spielzeug sowie Kindergartenbedarf, liegt in einem der Mieträume des Franziskanerklosters St. Columba. Größere Lager und Ausstellungsflächen für Kindergarten-Großgeräte befinden sich in Kellerräumen unter dem Hof.
Durch den Eingang gelangt man direkt in das Zentrum des Raums, in dem die Kasse und der Packtisch untergebracht sind. Im rechten Raumteil befinden sich auf der eingezogenen Galerie der Arbeitsplatz der Geschäftsführung und Beratungstische. Im darunter liegenden, extrem niedrigen Ladenteil werden Bücher und andere kleine Verkaufsartikel ausgestellt. Der linke Geschäftsteil hat eine normale Raumhöhe und ist mit einer Sitzgruppe ausgestattet.
Ein einfaches Baukastensystem dient der Präsentation des Verkaufsgutes: An sämtlichen Wänden sind Bohlen angebracht, die untereinander jeweils einen der Regalbodendicke entsprechenden Abstand halten. In diesen Schlitz werden die Regalböden eingeführt; durch eine entsprechende Profilierung des rückwärtigen Endes halten sie durch die Belastung mit der Ware ohne Beschläge.

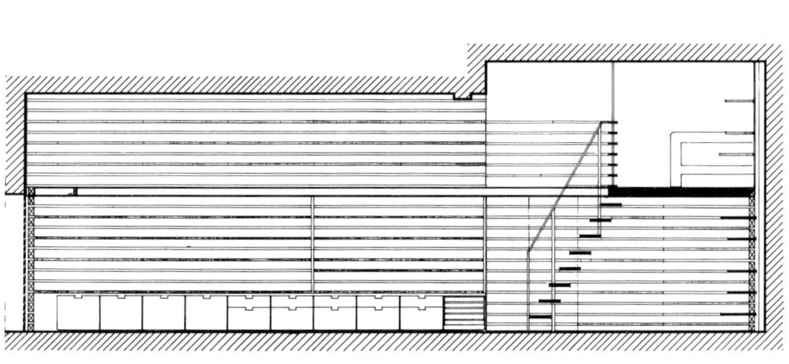
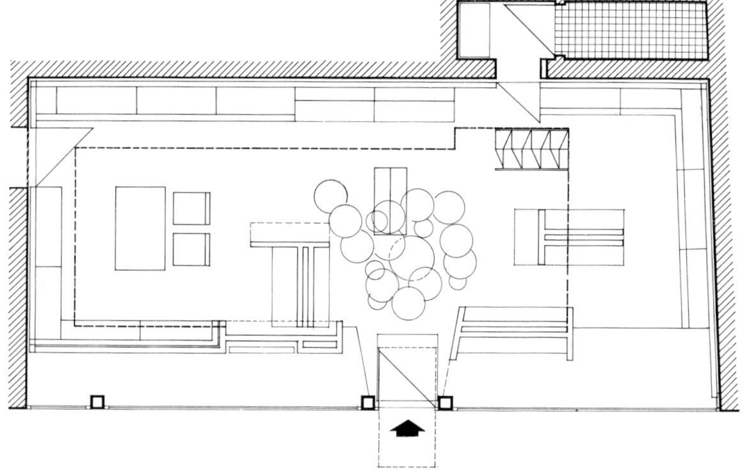

2

3

1. The shop fronts consist of movable elements. The door is a railway carriage door which opens automatically.
2. Plans (2nd basement, 1st basement, ground floor).
3. The characteristic atmosphere of the shop is created by its light, variable shape.

1. Die Ladenfronten bestehen aus beweglichen Elementen, die Tür ist eine sich automatisch öffnende Eisenbahntür.
2. Grundrisse (2. Untergeschoß, 1. Untergeschoß, Erdgeschoß).
3. Eine lockere, variable Gestalt gibt dem Laden seine spezifische Atmosphäre.

1

Incontro furnishing boutique, Berne

Architects: Remo G. Galli; assistants: Thomas Kühne and Edy Brunner

The characteristic atmosphere of Incontro, which is situated in the old part of Berne, is created by its light, variable shape — with the general tendency "to omit rather than obstruct".

The shop is 1.25–4.00 m in width, has a depth of 25 m and extends up three storeys (salesrooms on the ground floor and in the upper basement, storeroom in the lower basement). In the sales area no fixed ceiling was installed; instead, we find steel supports with sliding floor elements.

Eternit fixtures on wheels, movable wall bars as well as a goods and display paternoster lift, which can be operated by the customers themselves, are the principle elements of the variable interior arrangement which forms an unobtrusive background to the goods on display.

Einrichtungsboutique Incontro, Bern

Architekt: Remo G. Galli; Mitarbeiter: Thomas Kühne und Edy Brunner

Eine lockere, variable Gestalt — mit der Grundtendenz »Weglassen statt Verbauen« — gibt dem in der Berner Alstadt gelegenen Laden Incontro seine spezifische Atmosphäre.

Der Laden hat eine Breite von 1,25–4,00 m sowie eine Tiefe von 25 m und verfügt über drei Stockwerke (Verkaufsräume im Erdgeschoß und im 1. Untergeschoß, Lager im 2. Untergeschoß). Im Verkaufsbereich wurde keine feste Decke eingebaut; man entschied sich statt dessen für Stahlträger mit verschiebbaren Bodenelementen.

Rollbare Eternitgestelle, bewegliche Wandsprossen sowie ein Waren- und Ausstellungspaternoster, der vom Besucher bedient werden kann, bilden die wichtigsten Elemente der variablen Einrichtung, die gegenüber der ausgestellten Ware in den Hintergrund tritt.

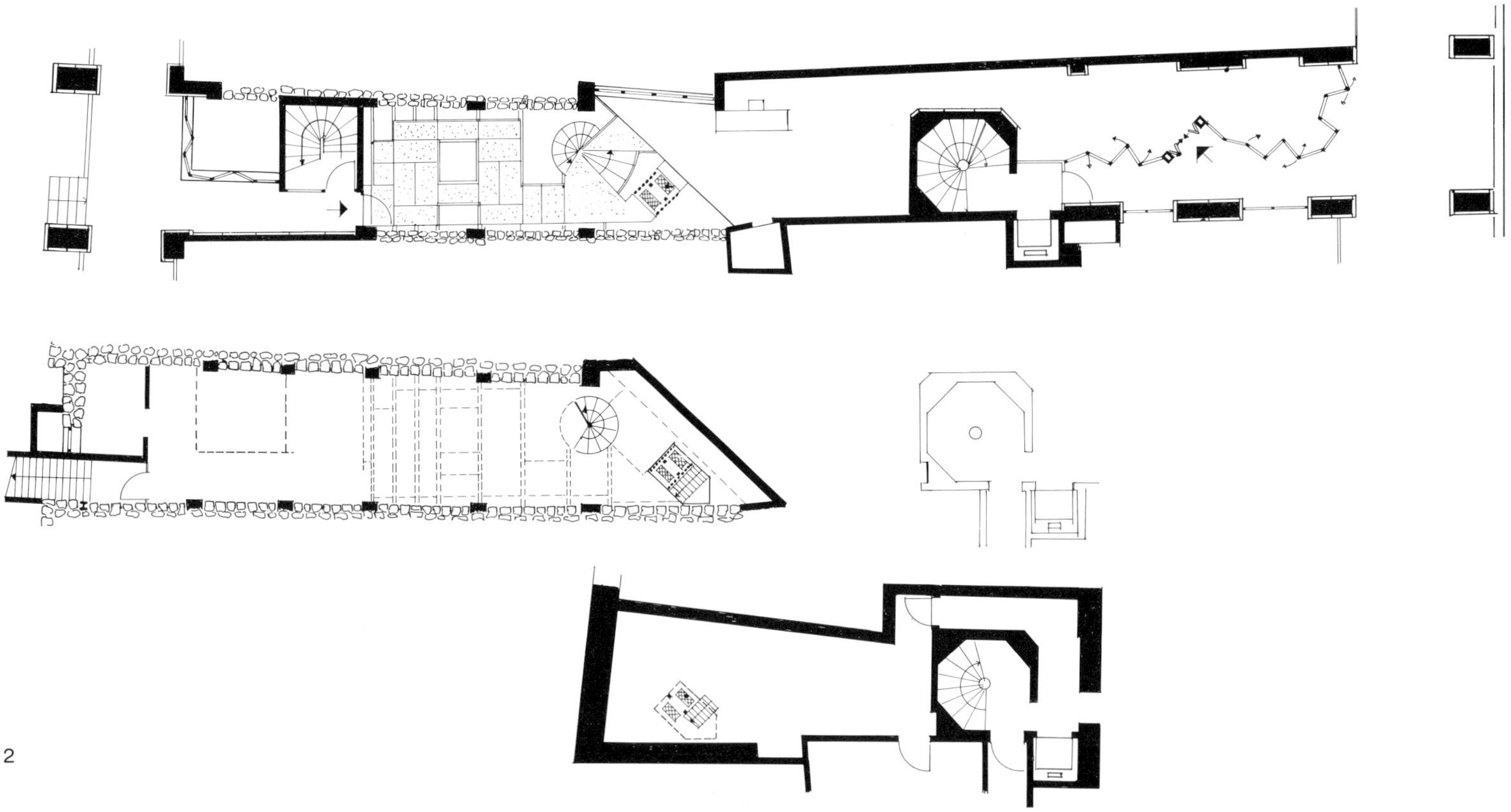

2

3

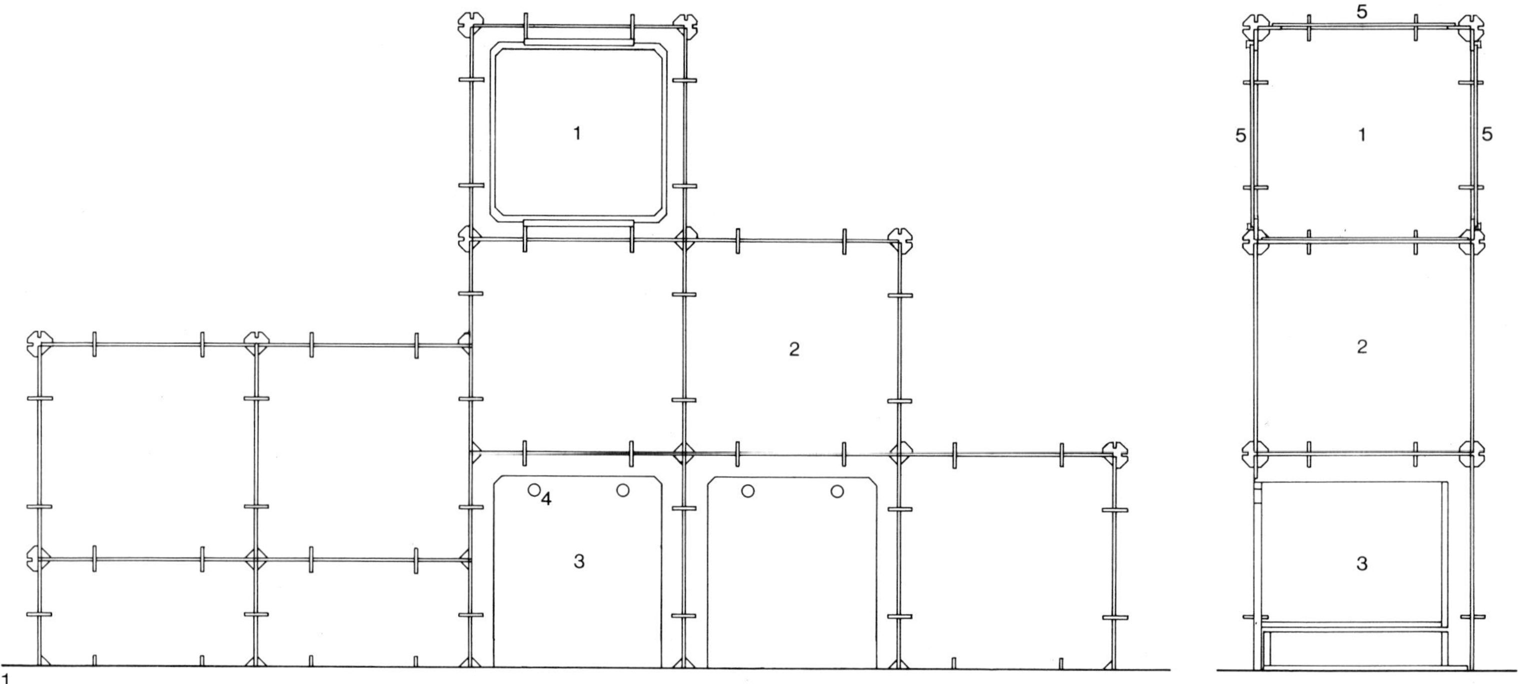

J. & L. Lobmeyr shop for furnishing requisites, Vienna
Architects: Karl and Eva Mang

The sales establishment of the Lobmeyr company had hardly been altered since its removal into Kärntner Strasse in 1885. In the course of conversion the entrance, which dates back to the era of Historicism, was retained in its original form, as was the typically 19th century sales area which extends up three storeys. During the reorganisation of the upper storeys nearly all structural parts remained unchanged or were renewed in the style of Historicism.

The showcases, the lighting and the cuboid elements of the seating group are constructed as variable elements. The white showcase units harmonize with the neutral background of the historicized forms, while the colours of the carpet and ceiling (red, blue, violet) form a sharp contrast to it.

The contrast between the 19th century architectural elements and the modern furnishings and lighting is also reflected in the company's sales programme.

Geschäft für Einrichtungsbedarf J. & L. Lobmeyr, Wien
Architekten: Karl und Eva Mang

Das Verkaufsgeschäft der Firma Lobmeyr war seit 1885, dem Jahr der Übersiedlung in die Kärtner Straße, kaum verändert worden. Beim Umbau blieb der Eingang aus der Zeit des Historismus ebenso in seiner ursprünglichen Form erhalten wie der über drei Stockwerke gehende Verkaufsraum, der typisch ist für das 19. Jahrhundert. Bei der Neugestaltung des obersten Stockwerks wurden praktisch alle Bauteile belassen oder im Sinn des Historismus erneuert.

Das Vitrinensystem, die Beleuchtung und die Würfelelemente der Sitzgruppe sind als variable Elemente ausgebildet. Das Weiß der Vitrinenelemente stimmt mit dem neutralen Hintergrund der historisierenden Formen überein, während die Farben des Teppichs und der Decke (rot, blau, violett) dazu in starkem Kontrast stehen.

Der Gegensatz zwischen den Architekturelementen des 19. Jahrhunderts und der modernen Möblierung und Beleuchtung spiegelt sich auch im Verkaufsprogramm der Firma.

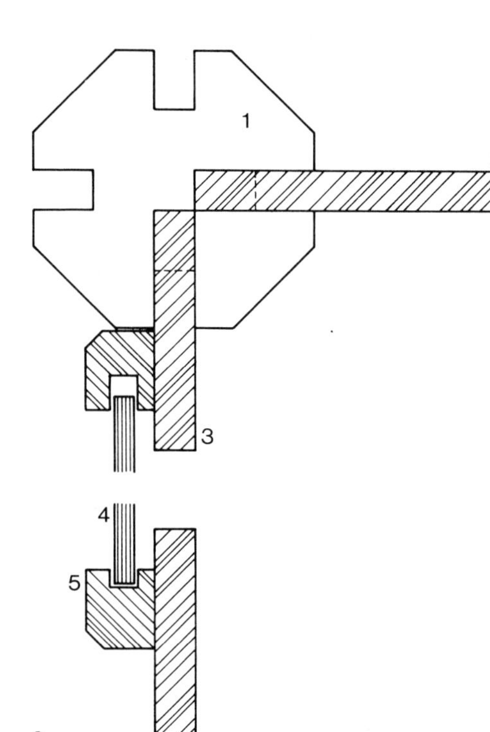

1. Detail of the showcase system (on the left elevation, on the right section). Key: 1 showcase, 2 closed element, 3 drawer, 4 hole for handling, 5 glass.
2. Detail of the sowcase. Key: 1 junction, 2 closed board element, 3 frame element for case window, 4 glass, 5 glass border.
3–5. Salesroom. The furnishings, which are constructed as variable elements, form a sharp constrast to the historicized forms of the background.

1. Detail des Vitrinensystems (links Ansicht, rechts Schnitt). Legende: 1 Vitrine, 2 volles Element, 3 Lade, 4 Griffloch, 5 Glas.
2. Vitrinendetail. Legende: 1 Verbindungsknoten, 2 volles Plattenelement, 3 Rahmenelement für Vitrinenfenster, 4 Glas, 5 Glasleiste.
3–5. Verkaufsraum. Die als variable Elemente ausgebildeten Einbauten stehen zu den historisierenden Formen der Raumhülle in einem starken Gegensatz.

1

Orthogonality furnishing boutique, Birmingham, Michigan
Architects: Steele + Bos

Orthogonality offers a wide range of merchandise which is characterized by an exceptional design (from toys to clothing, household articles and furniture).
A relatively high rectangular room was fitted with a gallery which is accessible by means of stairs varying in width and positioned at an angle of 45° to the front face. In addition to easing the traffic flow, this arrangement also establishes a complex spatial structure. The goods are displayed in such a way that an overall view of the entire range of articles is possible from the street. Since there are no shop-windows in the usual sense, the attention of passers-by is immediately drawn to the shop as a whole.
A particularly distinguishing feature of the shop is the yellow fibreglass entrance door which was made by a boatbuilder.

Einrichtungsboutique Orthogonality, Birmingham, Michigan
Architekten: Steele + Bos

Orthogonality ist ein Geschäft mit einem breiten Angebot von Waren, die sich durch ein vorbildliches Design auszeichnen (vom Spielzeug über Kleidung und Haushaltsartikel bis hin zu Möbeln).
Ein rechteckiger, relativ hoher Raum erhielt als Einbau eine Galerie, die über unterschiedlich breite Treppen zugänglich ist und unter einem Winkel von 45 Grad zur Vorderfront steht. Diese Anordnung führte nicht nur zu einer sinnvollen Wegführung, sondern ergab zugleich auch ein komplexes Raumgebilde. Die Waren sind so ausgestellt, daß der Betrachter von der Straße aus eine Übersicht über das gesamte Angebot erhält. Es gibt also keine Schaufenster im üblichen Sinn; die Aufmerksamkeit des Passanten wird vielmehr sogleich auf das Geschäft als Ganzes gelenkt.
Ein besonderes Kennzeichen des Geschäfts ist die Eingangstür aus gelbem Fiberglas, die von einem Bootsbauer hergestellt wurde.

2

1. View from outside into the shop. A particularly distinguishing feature is the yellow fibreglass entrance door.
2. Cashier area.
3. Axonometric view.
4. Access to the gallery is by two platforms which substantially contribute to the impression of a complex spatial structure.

1. Blick von außen in das Geschäft. Ein besonderes Kennzeichen ist die Eingangstür aus gelbem Fiberglas.
2. Kassenbereich.
3. Axonometrie.
4. Der Aufgang zur Galerie erfolgt über zwei breite Zwischenpodeste, die wesentlich zu dem Eindruck eines komplexen Raumgebildes beitragen.

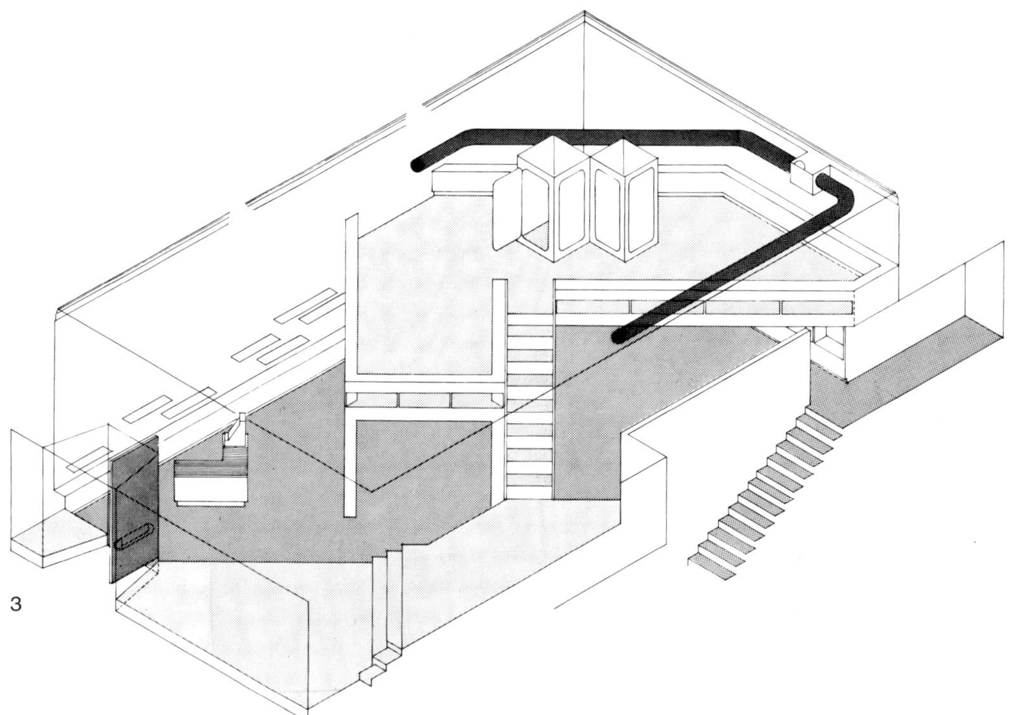

3

4

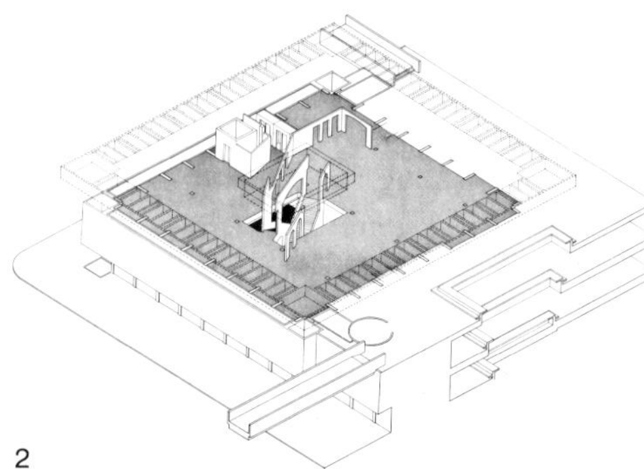

1

Design Research furnishing house, San Francisco
Architects: MLTW/Turnbull Associates

Design Research, a chain of shops specializing in the sale of furnishing requisites, opened its second shop in San Francisco in the Embarcadero Center, a large, grey megastructure in concrete with low, dark rooms.

In order to create a friendly atmosphere, a roof light, 5.5 × 8.5 m, was fitted over the central staircase. Its light falls on a stage-like setting of white walls whose openings are derived from the style of Victorian San Francisco. All technical equipment on the ceiling is covered with aluminium grids.

The basic concept behind the design was to create a large room which could be easily divided, and where the goods rather than the formal setting would be the focus of attraction for the buyer.

Einrichtungshaus Design Research, San Francisco
Architekten: MLTW / Turnbull Associates

Design Research, eine Ladenkette zum Verkauf von Einrichtungsbedarf, errichtete ihr zweites Geschäft in San Francisco im Embarcadero Center, einer großen, grauen Megastruktur aus Beton mit niedrigen, dunklen Räumen.

Um eine freundliche Atmosphäre zu erreichen, wurde ein 5,5 × 8,5 m großes Oberlicht über der zentralen Treppe angebracht, wobei das Licht auf kulissenartige weiße Wände fällt, die Öffnungen im Stil des viktorianischen San Francisco aufweisen. Alle technischen Einrichtungen an der Decke wurden mit Gitterrosten aus Aluminium abgedeckt.

Die grundsätzliche Überlegung zu der Gestaltung bestand darin, einen leicht zu unterteilenden Großraum zu schaffen, in dem sich der Käufer eher an den Waren als am formalen Rahmen vergnügt.

2

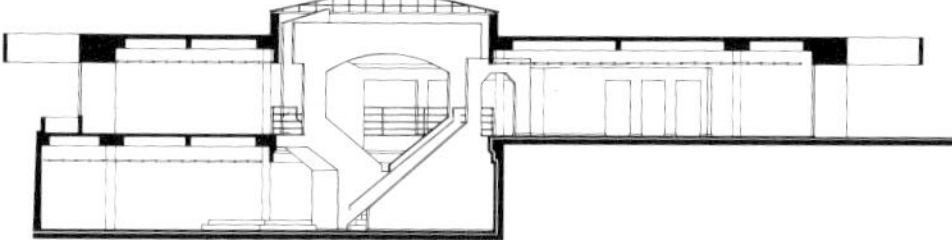

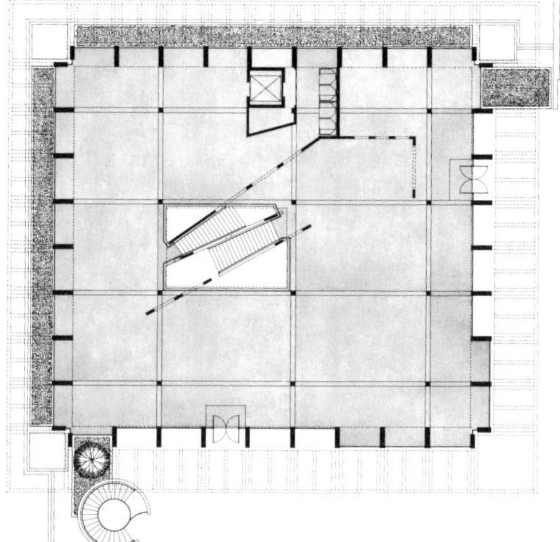

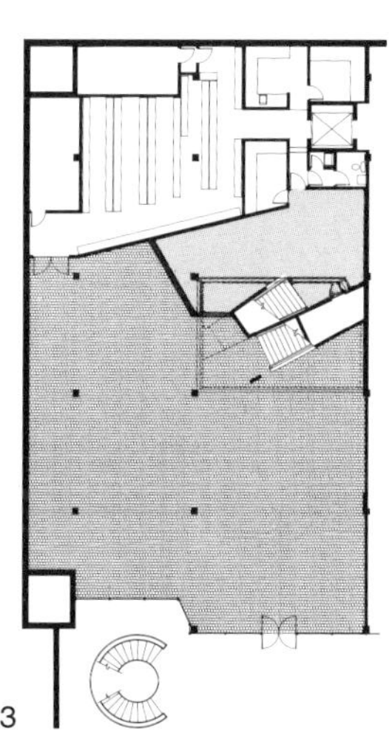

3

4

5

1. The main sales area on the upper floor is
a large room which could be easily divided.
2. Axonometric view of the upper-floor room.
3. Plans (lower floor, upper floor) and section.
4, 5. A roof-light, 5.5×8.5 m, was fitted over the
central staircase; its light falls on a stage-like
setting of white walls.

1. Die Hauptverkaufsfläche im Obergeschoß ist
ein leicht zu unterteilender Großraum.
2. Axonometrie des Obergeschoßraumes.
3. Grundrisse (Untergeschoß, Obergeschoß) und
Schnitt.
4, 5. Über der zentralen Treppe wurde ein 5,5×
8,5 m großes Oberlicht angebracht, wobei das
Licht auf kulissenartige weiße Wände fällt.

2

3

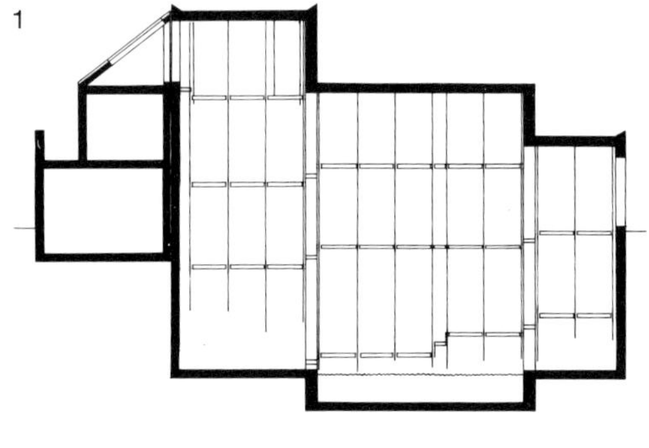
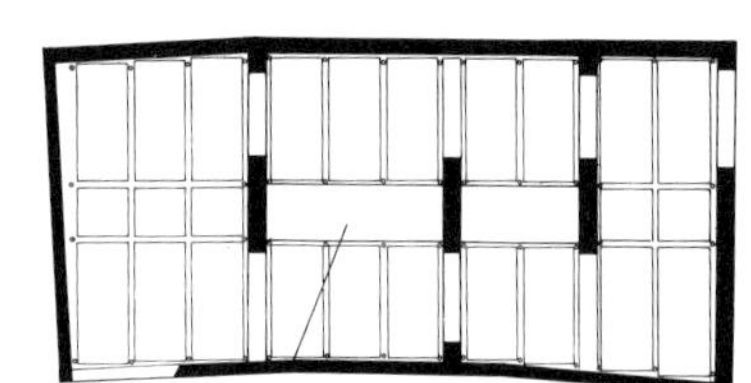

1

Extension of the furniture shop Neumarkt 17, Zurich
Architect: Fritz Schwarz

The design for the conversion of the furniture shop on the Zurich Neumarkt was based on the architect's theory that the correct interpretation of a place leads to a conclusive shape and that the project itself contributes to the design process in that it is an independent subject which impels solutions that comply with its inner purpose.

Since the 5.00 × 11.50 m site is built up on all sides, illumination was only possible from above. The cubic gradation to the narrow alley was necessary owing to the incidence of light, and consequently a tiered, sloping roof-light was fitted. The incidence of light from above lead to the use of transparent grids for the floors. In order to allow more light to enter the lower parts of the building, the floor was formed as a mirror surface; a water basin with circulation and filter prevents dust from settling on the mirrors.

Due to the small surface area and the incidence of light from above, it appeared necessary to emphasise the vertical lines. This was achieved with three massive piers. To maintain the visual continuity of these vertical lines, the mezzanines were suspended from the ceiling by adjustable steel chains. The mezzanines are arranged in the shape of a spiral, so that a separate staircase was unnecessary.

Anbau an das Möbelgeschäft Neumarkt 17, Zürich
Architekt: Fritz Schwarz

Dem Entwurf für den Anbau an das Möbelgeschäft am Züricher Neumarkt lag die Theorie des Architekten zugrunde, daß die richtige Interpretation eines Orts zu einer zwingenden Form führt, daß das Projekt selbst am Entwurfsvorgang beteiligt ist, indem es als selbständiges Subjekt zwingend zu Lösungen führt, die seinem inneren Sinn entsprechen.

Die ringsum eingebaute Parzelle von 5,00 × 11,50 m gestattete lediglich eine Belichtung von oben, die kubische Abstaffelung gegen die schmale Gasse war aus Gründen des Lichteinfalls nötig. Dadurch entstand ein treppenartig gestaffeltes, schräges Oberlicht. Der Lichteinfall von oben führte zu transparenten Gitterrosten als Böden. Um den Lichteinfall im unteren Gebäudeteil zu verstärken, wurde der Boden als Spiegelfläche ausgebildet; für den Schutz dieser Spiegel vor Verstaubung sorgt ein Wasserbassin mit Zirkulation und Filter.

Die kleine Grundfläche und der Lichteinfall von oben ließen eine Betonung der Vertikalen notwendig erscheinen, was mit drei wuchtigen Pfeilern geschah. Um diese durchgehenden Vertikalen optisch nicht zu stören, wurden die Zwischenböden mit Stahlketten – die verstellt werden können – an der Decke aufgehängt. Die Zwischenböden sind spiralförmig angeordnet, so daß sich eine gesonderte Treppe erübrigte.

1. Plan and section.
2. Since the 5.00 × 11.50 m site is built up on all sides, illumination was only possible from above.
3. View from inside towards the tiered, sloping roof-light.
4, 5. The incidence of light from above lead to the use of transparent grids for the floors. The mezzanines, which are suspended from the ceiling by chains, are arranged in the shape of a spiral, so that a separate staircase was unnecessary.

1. Grundriß und Schnitt.
2. Die ringsum eingebaute Parzelle von 5,00 × 11,50 m gestattete lediglich eine Belichtung von oben.
3. Blick von innen gegen das treppenartig gestaffelte, schräge Oberlicht.
4, 5. Der Lichteinfall von oben führte zu transparenten Gitterrosten als Böden. Die an Ketten aufgehängten Böden sind spiralförmig angeordnet, so daß sich eine gesonderte Treppe erübrigte.

4

5

1. The corner of the building with the entrance.
2. The shorter one of the two shop fronts. The entrance at the corner of the building is slightly recessed and accessible from both streets.
3. Plans (ground floor, upper floor) and sections. Key: 1 gallery, 2 salesroom, 3 showroom, 4 hole, 5 office, 6 WC, 7 wardrobe, 8 court, 9 void above the office.
4. View from the upper floor towards the entrance.
5. The stairs to the upper floor.
6. The large showroom on the ground floor.

1. Gebäudeecke mit Eingang.
2. Die kürzere der beiden Ladenfronten. Der an der Gebäudeecke liegende Eingang ist etwas zurückgesetzt und von beiden Straßen aus zugänglich.
3. Grundrisse (Erdgeschoß, Obergeschoß) und Schnitte. Legende: 1 Passage, 2 Verkaufsraum, 3 Schauraum, 4 Grube, 5 Büro, 6 WC, 7 Garderobe, 8 Hof, 9 Luftraum Büro.
4. Blick vom Obergeschoß auf den Eingang.
5. Der Aufgang zum Obergeschoß.
6. Der große Ausstellungsraum im Erdgeschoß.

Section N furniture shop, Vienna

Architect: Hans Hollein; assistants: Gerd Dinklage, Helmut Grasberger and Helga Singer

The Section N furniture shop occupies part of the old Neubergerhof, which, in its present form, dates from the late Baroque period. It is used for the sale and rental of furniture and other household articles, avant-garde in their design.

In the course of the conversion the original building structure was exposed and retained as far as possible. Depending on functional requirements, built-in units were set into the existing framework; among them a mezzanine, the form of which clearly contrasts with the other building elements, was added to compensate for the limited space. The succession of spaces was deliberately designed in such a way that the different levels could be linked by short staircases and small intermediate landings. In this way, it was possible to create a sequence of inter-related rooms, which not only vary in size but also offer a large variety of display and service areas.

Intentionally simple in its design, the materials and colouring of the interior create an atmosphere reminiscent of the Vienna of the past.

Möbelgeschäft Section N, Wien

Architekt: Hans Hollein; Mitarbeiter: Gerd Dinklage, Helmut Grasberger und Helga Singer

Das Möbelgeschäft Section N nimmt einen Teil des alten Neubergerhofs ein, dessen heutige Bausubstanz aus der Zeit des Spätbarock stammt. Es dient dem Verkauf und der Vermietung von Möbeln und anderen Einrichtungsgegenständen avantgardistischen Zuschnitts.

Beim Umbau wurde die alte Bausubstanz so weit wie möglich wieder freigelegt beziehungsweise erhalten. In dieses vorhandene Grundgerüst kamen je nach funktionaler Erfordernis Einbauten, darunter wegen der geringen zur Verfügung stehenden Fläche ein Zwischengeschoß, welches sich in seiner Form klar von den übrigen Bauteilen absetzt. Die räumliche Abfolge wurde bewußt so gestaltet, daß die Überwindung der Höhenunterschiede mit nur kurzen Treppenläufen und kleinen Zwischenpodesten vorgenommen werden konnte. Es entstand so ein Ablauf ineinanderfließender Räume wechselnder Größe mit einer Vielzahl unterschiedlicher Präsentationsflächen und Bereiche.

Gestaltungsmäßig wurde bewußt mit einfachen Mitteln gearbeitet, die – etwa in bezug auf Materialwahl und Farbgebung – eine dem Altwienerischen nicht unähnliche Stimmung erzeugen.

4

5

3

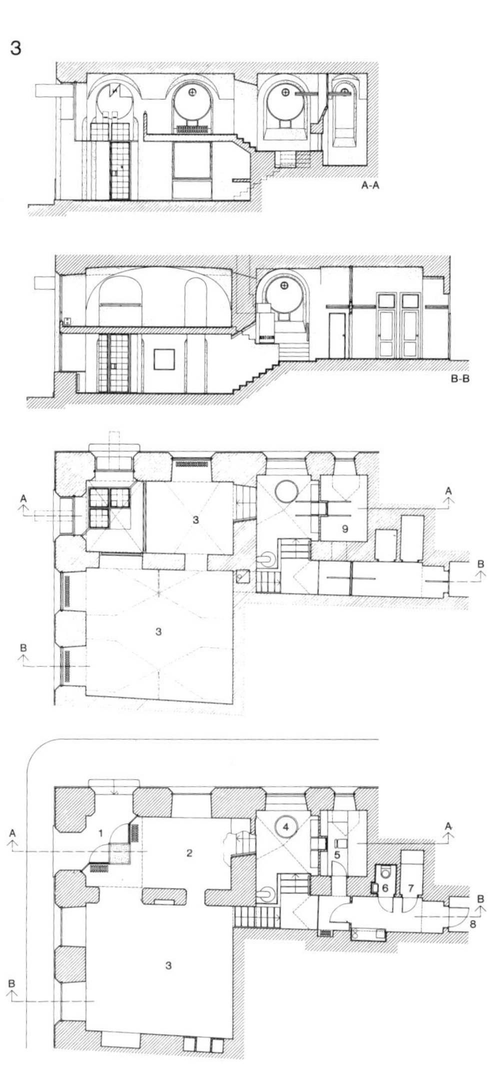

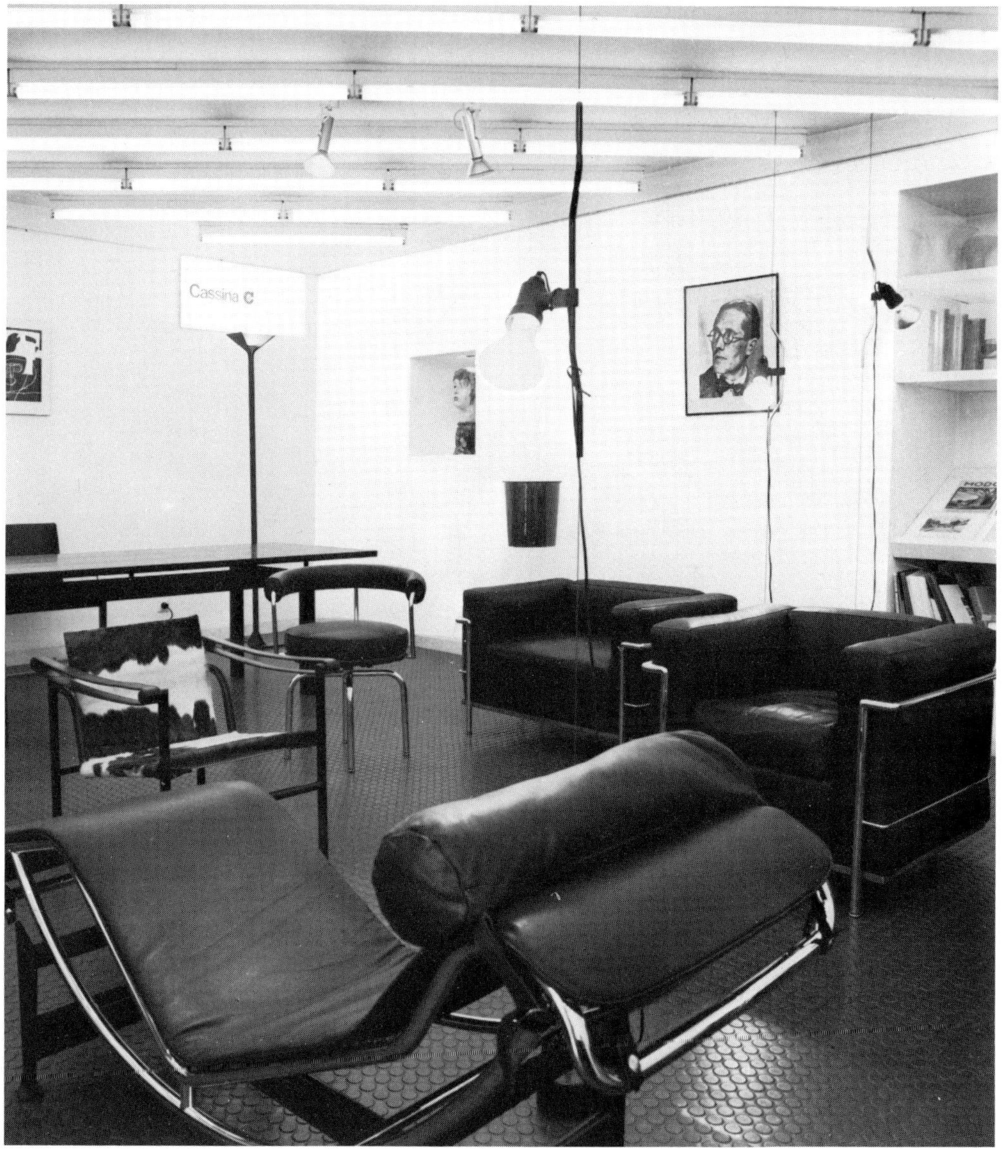

6

2

1

Lanaro company furniture display rooms, Vicenza
Architects: Lanaro Arredamenti

The rooms of the Lanaro company, which are situated on the Corso San Felice and serve as display areas for furniture, were accommodated in the church of San Valentino and in the neighbouring building to its left.
The church had long since been given over to secular usage and had been used as a storeroom, for which purpose mezzanines had been inserted in the aisles. In the course of conversion, the mezzanines were retained, while the nave was restored to its original state. The upper levels of the aisles were separated from the nave by thin cables which were stretched at close intervals between roof and mezzanine.
While removing the plaster coat from the old walls, 18th century frescoes were uncovered. Although of no particular artistic value, with their soft grey and ochre colouring they form a pleasant background to the modern furnishings.

Ausstellungsräume für Möbel der Firma Lanaro, Vicenza
Architekten: Lanaro Arredamenti

Die am Corso San Felice gelegenen und der Präsentation von Büromöbeln dienenden Räume der Firma Lanaro wurden in der Kirche San Valentino und deren links davon gelegenem Nachbargebäude eingerichtet.
Die Kirche war bereits vor längerer Zeit dem profanen Gebrauch überlassen worden und wurde bisher als Lagerraum benutzt, wofür man in den Seitenschiffen Zwischendecken eingeschoben hatte. Während man diese Zwischendecken bestehen ließ, versetzte man das Mittelschiff wieder in seinen ursprünglichen Zustand. Die obere Ebene der Seitenschiffe wurde gegen das Mittelschiff durch dünne Seile abgetrennt, die man in engem Abstand zwischen Dach- und Zwischendecke spannte.
Bei der Entfernung der Putzschicht auf den alten Mauern kamen Fresken aus dem 18. Jahrhundert zum Vorschein. Obwohl es sich dabei um keine besonders wertvollen Werke handelt, bilden sie mit ihren zarten Grau- und Ockertönen doch einen angenehmen Hintergrund für die moderne Einrichtung.

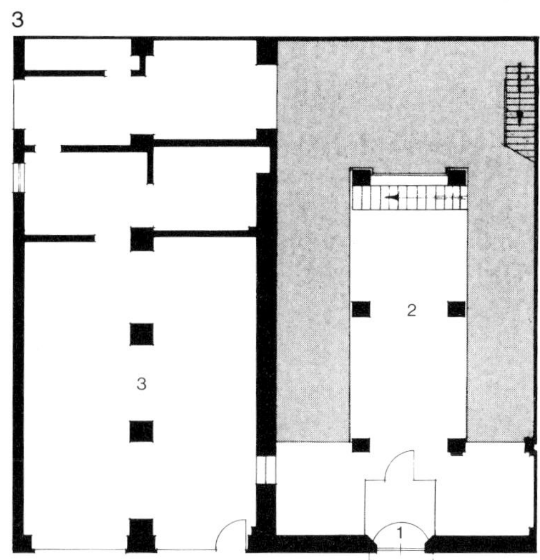

1. The anteroom of the former church with the main entrance.
2. Street front. Lanaro occupies not only the former church but also the neighbouring building to the left.
3. Plan (ground floor). Key: 1 main entrance, 2 the former church, 3 the neighbouring building to the left.
4. While removing the plaster coat from the old walls, 18th century frescoes were uncovered.
5. The interior of the former church, looking towards the street.

1. Der Vorraum der ehemaligen Kirche mit dem Haupteingang.
2. Straßenfront. Lanaro beansprucht neben der ehemaligen Kirche auch das links anschließende Nachbargebäude.
3. Grundriß (Erdgeschoß). Legende: 1 Haupteingang, 2 ehemalige Kirche, 3 linkes Nachbargebäude.
4. Bei der Entfernung der Putzschicht auf den alten Mauern kamen Fresken aus dem 18. Jahrhundert zum Vorschein.
5. Der Raum der ehemaligen Kirche in Richtung Straße.

1

Luz butcher's shop, Stuttgart-Bad Cannstatt
Architects: Werner Luz; assistants: Helmut Rabien, Jobst Roselius and Axel Asseburg

Situated in the Marktstrasse in the old part of Bad Cannstatt, Luz butcher's shop is accommodated in a building which was erected in 1948 and comprises two main floors and an attic. The previous stationer's shop on the ground floor had a conventional structural layout: The first level was almost 1 m above that of the Marktstrasse, and the central entrance had shop-windows to the left and right.
By lowering the shop level to that of the street, and introducing floor-to-ceiling glazing, an attempt was made to blend the new shop into its surroundings.
The sales area is divided into two parts and comprises the square-shaped salesrooms of the actual butcher's shop in the Marktstrasse as well as the long, narrow stand-up snack bar on the "Kunsthöfle".

2

Metzgerei Luz, Stuttgart-Bad Cannstatt
Architekt: Werner Luz; Mitarbeiter: Helmut Rabien, Jobst Roselius und Axel Asseburg

Die Metzgerei Luz, an der Marktstraße in der Cannstatter Altstadt gelegen, wurde in einem 1948 errichteten Gebäude mit zwei Hauptgeschossen und einem Dachgeschoß eingerichtet. Im Erdgeschoß befand sich früher ein Papierwarengeschäft mit konventionellem baulichen Zuschnitt: das Niveau fast 1 m über der Marktstraße, Mitteleingang mit rechts und links davon angeordneten Schaufenstern.
Durch Absenken der Ladenebene auf das Straßenniveau und Vollverglasung wurde der neue Laden so weit wie möglich in den Straßenraum eingebunden.
Der Verkaufsbereich besteht aus zwei Teilen, dem an der Marktstraße gelegenen quadratischen Kundenraum der eigentlichen Metzgerei sowie dem längsgerichteten Stehimbiß am »Kunsthöfle«.

1. The front of the shop on the Marktstrasse.
2. Sales counter.
3. Plan. Key: 1 customers' area, 2 cash desk,
3 sales, 4 stand-up snack bar, 5 delivery,
6 refrigerated room.
4. The stand-up snack bar on the Kunsthöfle.

1. Die Front zur Marktstraße.
2. Verkaufstheke.
3. Grundriß. Legende: 1 Kundenraum, 2 Kasse.
3 Verkauf, 4 Stehimbiß, 5 Anlieferung,
6 Kühlraum.
4. Stehimbiß am »Kunsthöfle«.

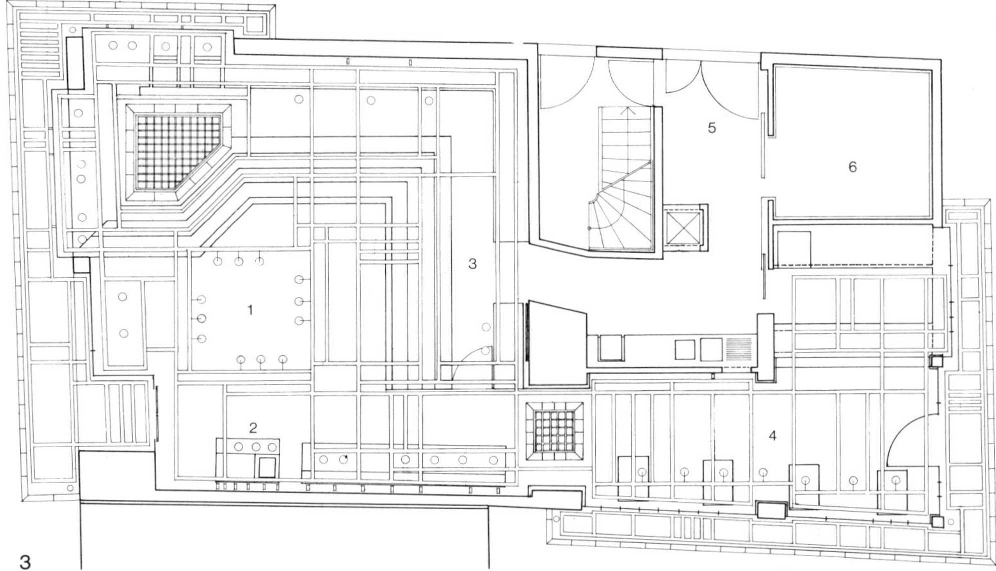

3

4

1

Burkhardt bakery, Volketswil shopping centre, near Zurich
Architect: Gerd Burla

As opposed to the traditional baker's shop in which the bakery wares are surrounded by wood and cloth (materials closely related to them) in this shop steel plate, synthetic resin and ceramic, brownish violet in colour, together with chrome steel and glass form the background for the displayed goods. Owing to the unobtrusive decoration and the omission of natural materials, the full diversity of the bakery products is accentuated.

Bäckerei Burkhardt, Einkaufszentrum Volketswil bei Zürich
Architekt: Gerd Burla

Im Gegensatz zum traditionellen Bäckerladen, der das Backgut mit Holz und Stoff umgibt – mit Materialien, die diesem sehr verwandt sind –, bilden bei diesem Laden Stahlblech, Kunstharz und Keramik, in der Farbe braunviolett, zusammen mit Chromstahl und Glas den Hintergrund der ausgestellten Ware. Durch Zurückhaltung in der Verwendung von Dekor und durch den Verzicht auf lebendiges Material wird die Erscheinung des Backguts in seiner ganzen Differenziertheit hervorgehoben.

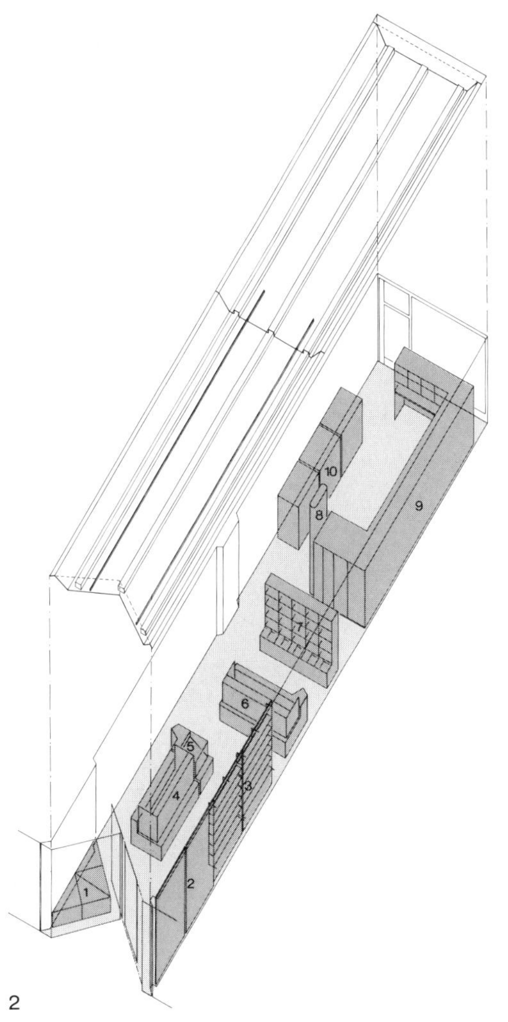

2

3

4

1. View from the entrance into the salesroom.
2. Axonometric view. Key: 1 shop-window, 2 mobile photo board, 3 mobile presentation stand for chocolate, 4 refrigerated showcase for fancy cakes, 5 refrigerated showcase for chocolates, 6 refrigerated showcase for small loaves and pastry, 7 bread stand, 8 electric supply, 9 office, 10 refrigerated boxes.
3. Shopping arcade. The bakery is in front on the left.
4. Display of bread in front of the photo board.

1. Blick vom Eingang in den Verkaufsraum.
2. Axonometrie. Legende: 1 Schaufenster, 2 mobile Photowand, 3 mobiles Präsentationsgestell für Schokolade, 4 Kühlvitrine für Torten, 5 Kühlvitrine für Pralinen, 6 Kühlvitrine für Kleinbrot und Gebäck, 7 Brotgestell, 8 Elektrozentrale, 9 Büro, 10 Kühlboxen.
3. Ladenpassage. Vorn links die Bäckerei.
4. Präsentation von Brot vor der mobilen Photowand.

1. Site plan. Below the town hall, above the cheese shop.
2. View from the town-hall passage towards the shop.
3. The building which houses the shop has a symmetrical Baroque façade.

1. Lageplan. Unten die Rathauspassage, oben das Käsegeschäft.
2. Blick von der Rathauspassage auf den Laden.
3. Das Gebäude, in dem sich das Geschäft befindet, hat eine symmetrisch aufgebaute Fassade aus der Zeit des Barock.

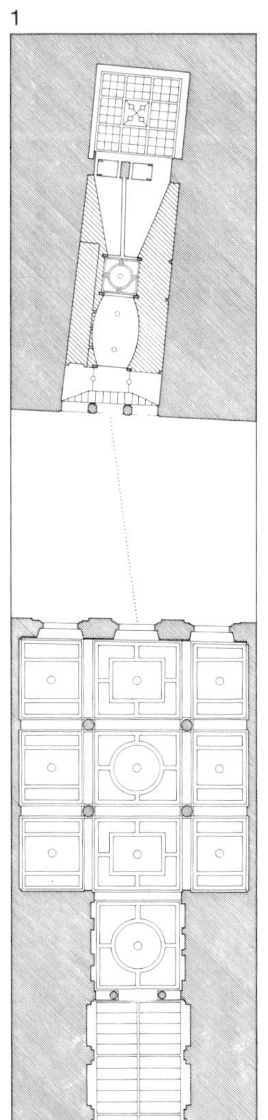

1

2

3

Chäs-Küde cheese shop, Winterthur
Architect: Arnold Amsler; assistant: Vrendli Amsler

When converting the shop, situated in the old part of Winterthur, the architect was guided by two factors: the symmetrical Baroque façade of the building in which it is accommodated, and the 19th century town-hall passage directly opposite.
The façade itself remained unaltered; the shop front curves slightly inward behind the two piers which bear the weight of the upper storeys. This perspective extension is simultaneously a spatial response to the aperture of the town-hall passage opposite. The very narrow, 20 m deep shop interior is designed in such a way that it is experienced as a continuation of the passage. A series of differently shaped rooms are joined together along an axis: The shop-window, divided into small panes, is followed by an oblong oval room. This is followed by a square-shaped room with stuccoed ceiling which forms the actual centre of the shop. From here one comes to a triangular room with a free-standing archway. The room series ends with a bright, covered courtyard.

Käsegeschäft Chäs-Küde, Winterthur
Architekt: Arnold Amsler; Mitarbeiterin: Vrendli Amsler

Beim Umbau des in der Winterthurer Altstadt gelegenen Geschäfts ließ sich der Architekt von zwei Gegebenheiten leiten: von der symmetrisch aufgebauten Barockfassade des Gebäudes, das das Geschäft beherbergt, sowie von der gegenüberliegenden Rathauspassage aus dem 19. Jahrhundert.
Die Fassade selbst blieb völlig intakt; die Schaufensterfront buchtet hinter den zwei Pfeilern, die die Lasten von den Obergeschossen tragen, leicht zurück. Diese perspektivische Ausweitung ist zugleich auch als räumliche Antwort auf die Mündung des Rathausdurchgangs gegenüber zu verstehen. Das 20 m tiefe, aber sehr schmale Ladeninnere wurde so gestaltet, daß man es als Fortsetzung der Passage erlebt. Axial sind verschiedene Raumformen hintereinandergeschaltet: Auf die feingliedrige Schaufensteranlage folgt ein längsgerichteter ovaler Raum. Diesem schließt sich ein an der Decke stuckierter quadratischer Raum an, der das Zentrum des Ladens bildet. Von hier geht es weiter in einen dreieckigen Raum mit einem frei stehenden Torbogen als Abschluß. Das Ende der Raumfolge bildet ein lichter Hofraum.

4. The shop front curves slightly inwards behind
the two piers.
5. Axonometric view.

4. Die Schaufensterfront buchtet hinter den zwei
Pfeilern leicht zurück.
5. Axonometrie.

4

5

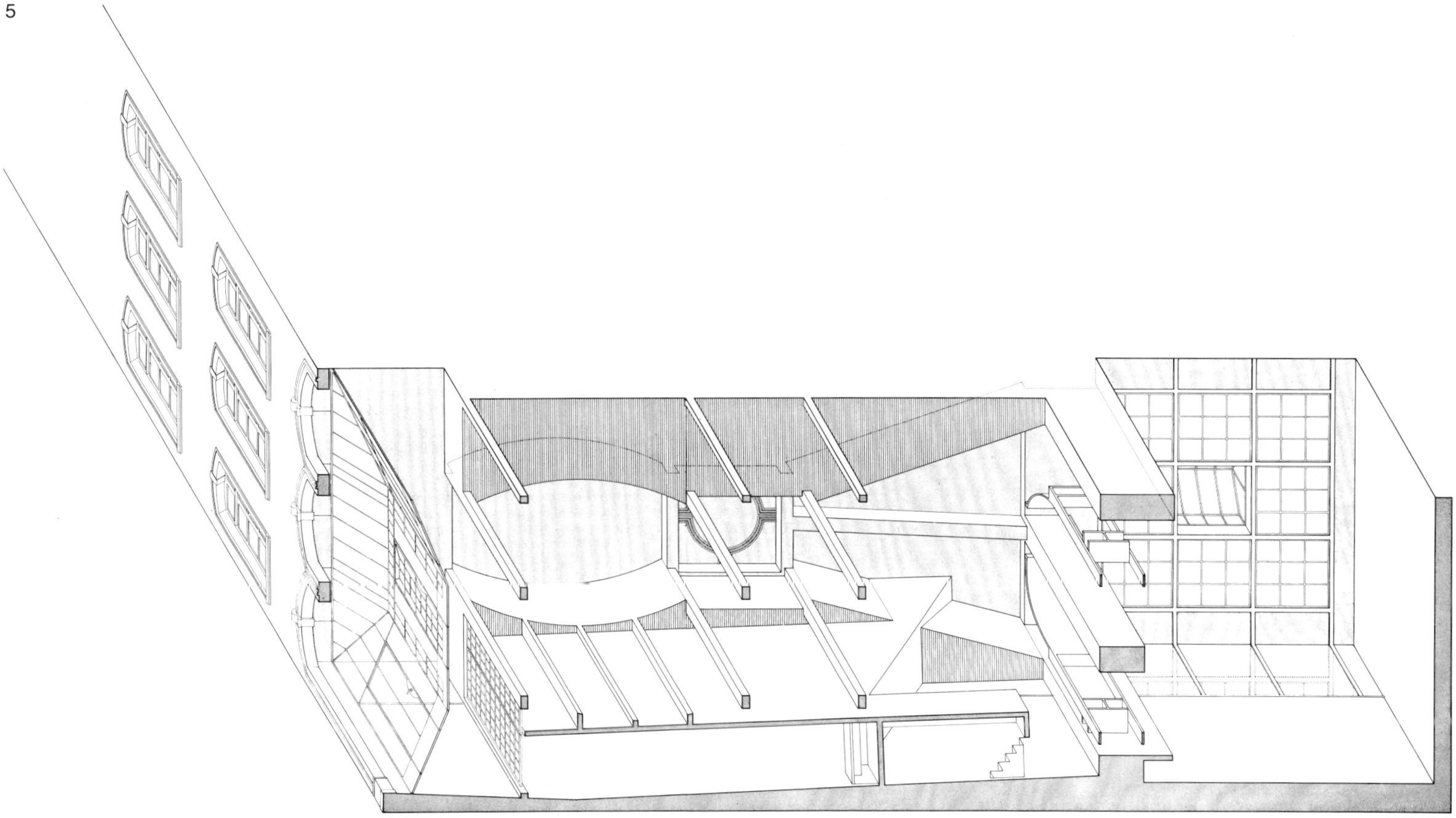

6. The oval room behind the shop-window construction.
7. View from the square-shaped room towards the entrance.
8. View from the oval room towards the entrance.

6. Der ovale Raum hinter der Schaufensteranlage.
7. Blick vom quadratischen Raum in Richtung Eingang.
8. Blick vom ovalen Raum auf den Eingang.

1. Model.

1. Modell.

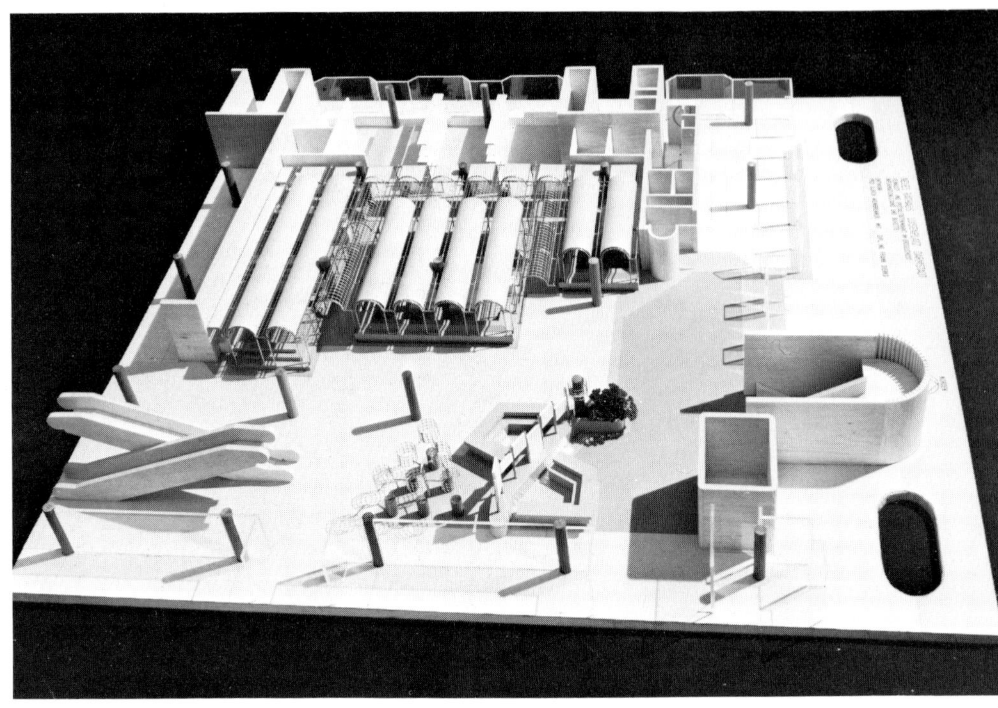

1

Delicatessen shop market in the Neues Rathaus in Darmstadt
Architects: Ulrich Weinbrenner and Frank Dierks

Ten delicatessen shops were to be accommodated in an area 650 m² on the ground floor of the Neues Rathaus on the Luisenplatz. A pedestrian gallery leads onto one side of the virtually square area. The head room is 3.60 m.
In accordance with the client's wishes, the shop area has a uniform appearance which emphasizes the diversity of the range of merchandise and promotes the lively sales activity characteristic of a "market hall".
Access from the main gallery to the delicatessen market is gained by way of a U-shaped side-street whose rear section expands to form a small square. This arrangement produces a central group, and rows of shops along the marginal areas. The spatial shells, which are adapted to the range of merchandise of the individual shops and stalls, are uniform and neutral in their design, thus offering the tenants the possibility of realizing their own concepts of an interior arrangement.

Feinkost-Fachgeschäftemarkt im Neuen Rathaus in Darmstadt
Architekten: Ulrich Weinbrenner und Frank Dierks

Zehn Spezialitätengeschäfte waren auf einer Grundfläche von 650 m² im Erdgeschoß des Neuen Rathauses am Luisenplatz unterzubringen. Die nahezu quadratisch zugeschnittene Fläche wird einseitig von einer Fußgängerpassage tangiert. Die lichte Raumhöhe beträgt 3,60 m.
Entsprechend den Vorstellungen des Bauherrn wurde dem Ladenbereich ein einheitliches Erscheinungsbild gegeben, das die Vielfalt des Warenangebots voll zur Geltung bringt und die Lebendigkeit des Verkaufsgeschehens im Sinn einer »Markthalle« erlebbar macht.
Von der Hauptpassage aus wird der Feinkostmarkt durch eine U-förmig angeordnete Seitenstraße erschlossen, die sich im hinteren Bereich platzartig erweitert. Daraus ergibt sich eine mittig liegende Ladengruppe und eine Reihung entlang der Randzonen. Die auf das Warenangebot der einzelnen Läden und Stände abgestimmten, ansonsten einheitlich und neutral gestalteten Raumhüllen geben den Pächtern die Möglichkeit, individuelle Ausbauvorstellungen zu verwirklichen.

2. Delicatessen stall.
3. Florist's studio.
4. Fruit and vegetable stall.

2. Feinkoststand.
3. Floristik-Studio.
4. Obst- und Gemüsestand.

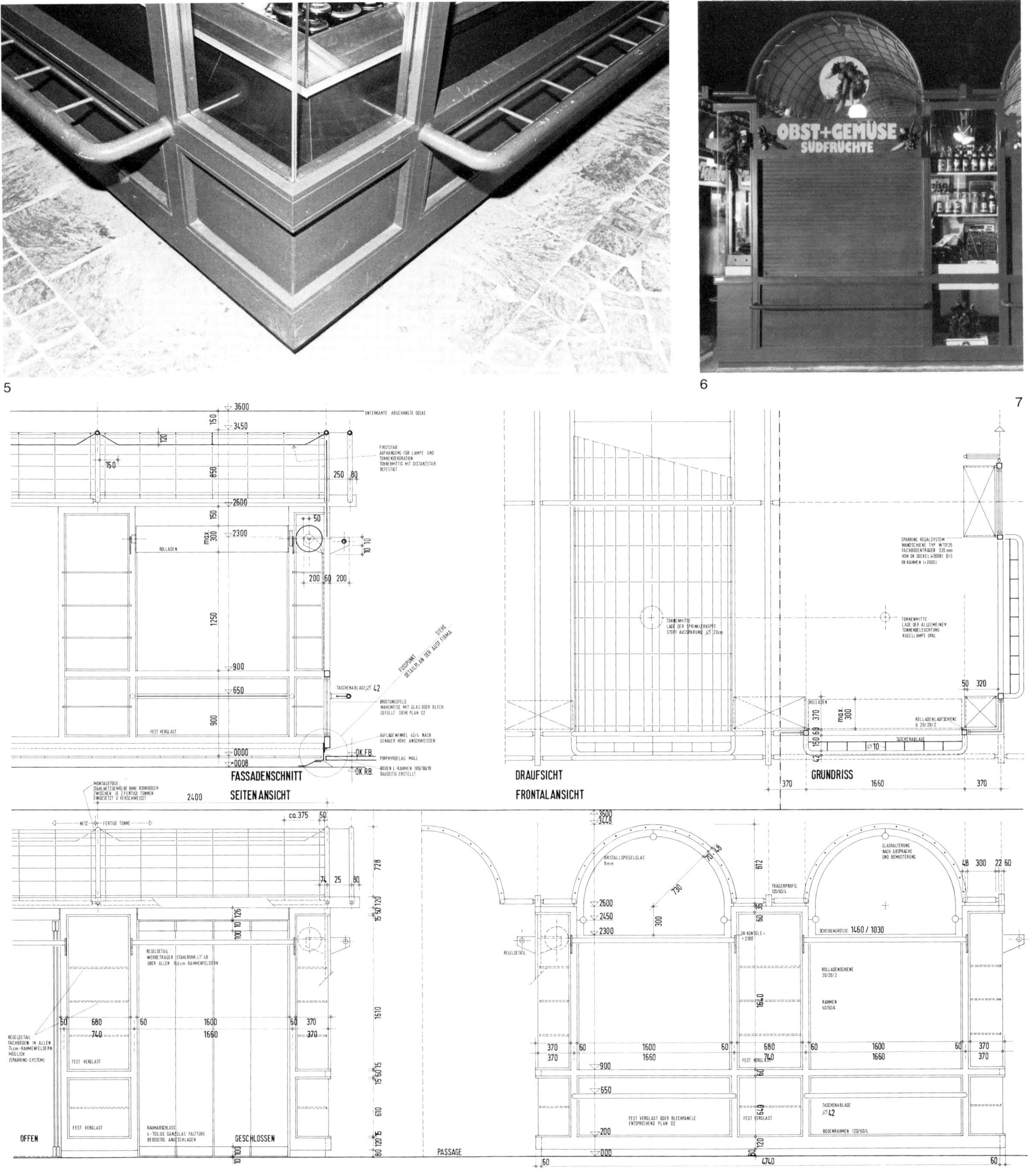
OBST + GEMÜSE
SÜDFRÜCHTE
5
6
7
FASSADENSCHNITT
SEITENANSICHT
DRAUFSICHT
FRONTALANSICHT
GRUNDRISS
OFFEN
GESCHLOSSEN
PASSAGE
ROLLADEN
FEST VERGLAST
TASCHENABLAGE
UNTERKANTE ABGEHANGTE DECKE
O.K.FB.
O.K.RB.

5. Outside corner of a stall.
6. One field of the fruit and vegetable stall in closed position.
7. Details of the stall construction (section through the façade, top view and plan, side elevation, front elevation).
8. Plan. Access from the main gallery to the delicatessen market is gained by way of a U-shaped side-street. This arrangement produces a central group and rows of shops along the marginal areas.
9. View from the main gallery towards the delicatessen market.

5. Außenecke eines Stands.
6. Ein Feld des Obst- und Gemüsestands in geschlossenem Zustand.
7. Details der Standkonstruktion (Fassadenschnitt, Aufsicht und Grundriß, Seitenansicht, Frontalansicht).
8. Grundriß. Von der Hauptpassage aus wird der Feinkostmarkt durch eine U-förmig angeordnete Seitenstraße erschlossen. Daraus ergibt sich eine mittig liegende Ladengruppe und eine Reihung entlang der Randzonen.
9. Blick von der Hauptpassage auf den Feinkostmarkt.

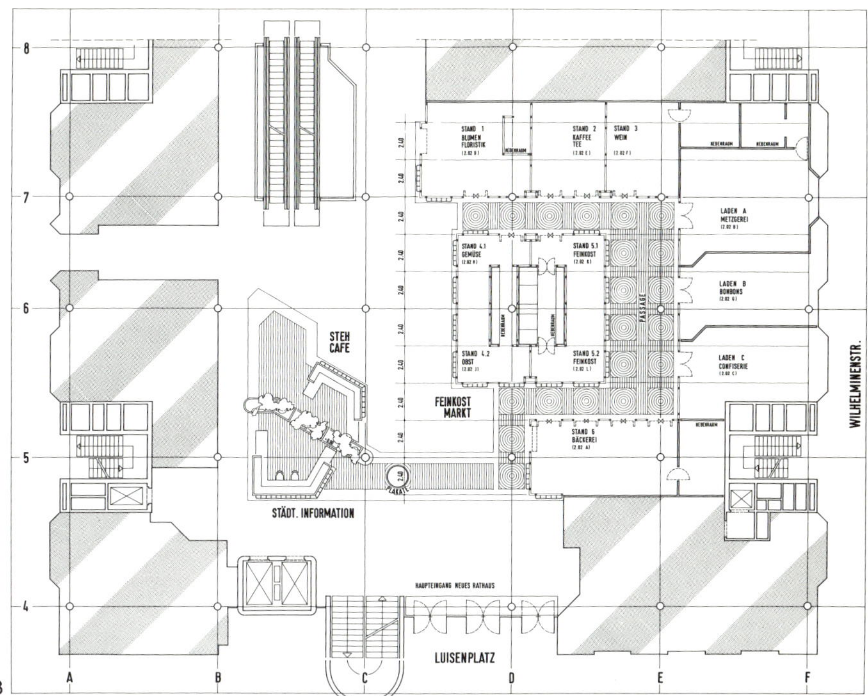

8

9

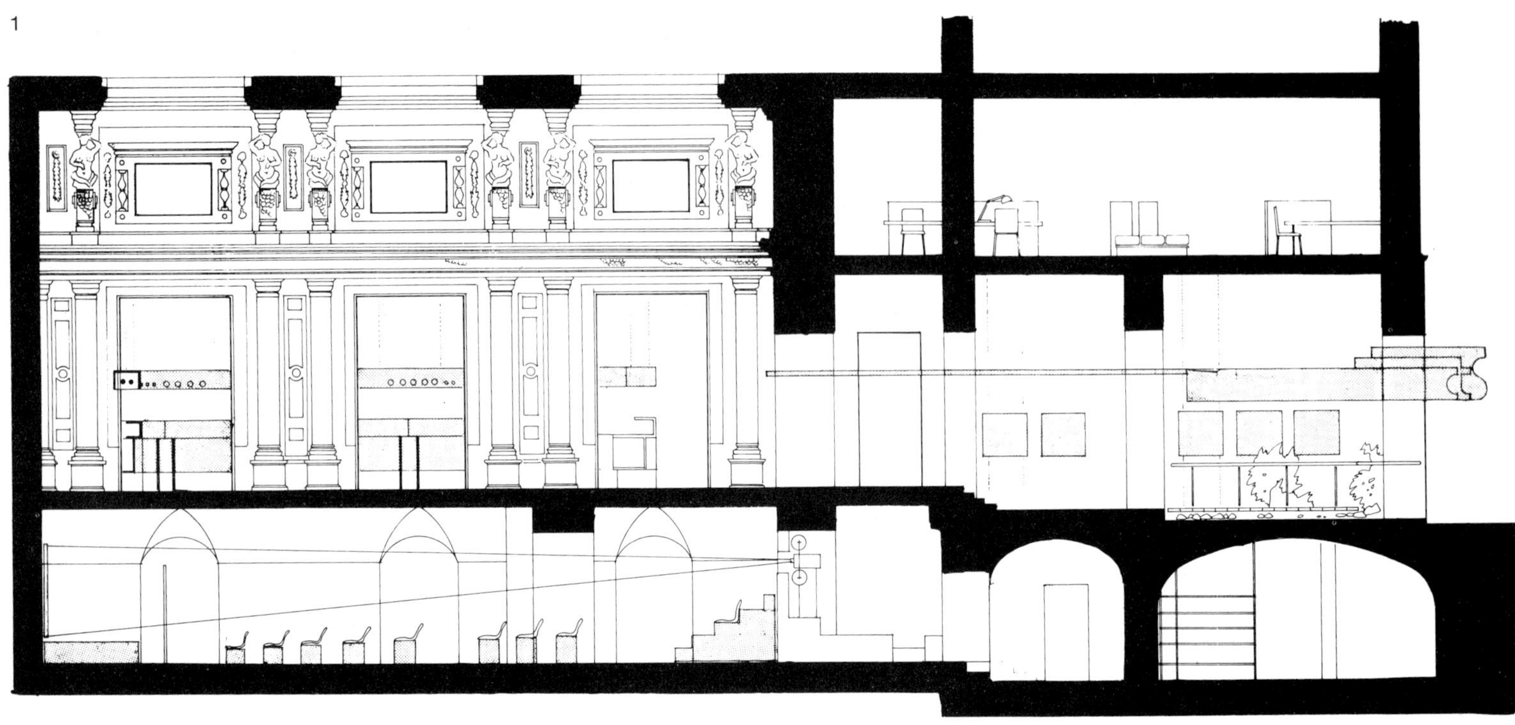

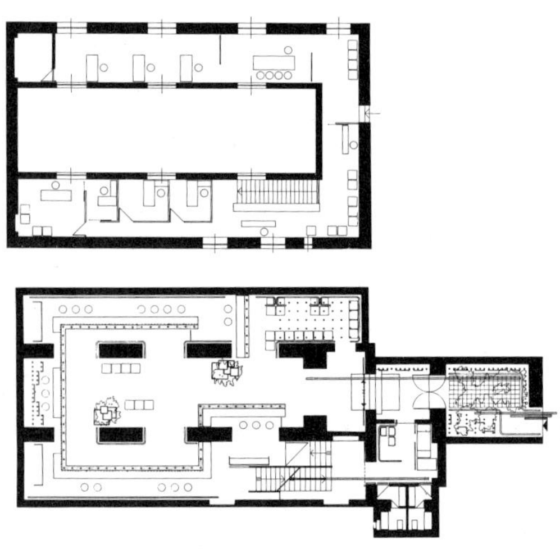

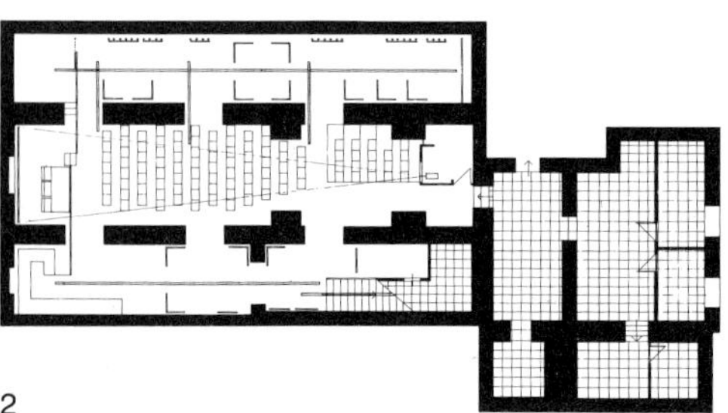

C.T.S. student travel centre, Rome

Architects: Tullio Leonori, Luca Leonori and Piero Gandolfi

The new headquarters of the C.T.S. (Centro Turistico Studentesco) is accommodated in a palazzo on the Via Nazionale.

The centre of the building is a richly decorated hall which is flanked by narrower rooms on the long sides. Owing to its marked articulation, the hall, which receives daylight through three roof-lights, takes on a street-like character. This is further accentuated by the intensive colouring as well as by the furnishing elements (street lighting, benches, flooring of moulded rubber, plants). The service counters form a compact white band which winds its way through the rooms without interfering with the original structure.

A conference room with 100 seats and display areas to the left and right is accommodated below the hall.

Studentenreisezentrum C.T.S., Rom

Architekten: Tullio Leonori, Luca Leonori und Piero Gandolfi

Der neue Sitz des C.T.S. (Centro Turistico Studentesco) befindet sich in einem Palazzo an der Via Nazionale.

Zentrum des Gebäudes ist eine reich verzierte Halle, die an den Längsseiten von schmaleren Räumen flankiert wird. Durch ihre stark betonte Gliederung hat die Halle, die über drei große Oberlichter Tageslicht erhält, Straßencharakter, der sowohl durch die intensive Farbgebung als auch durch die Einrichtungselemente (Straßenbeleuchtung, Bänke, profilierter Gummiboden, Pflanzen) zusätzlich hervorgehoben wird. Die Abfertigungsschalter ziehen sich als kompaktes weißes Band durch die Räume, ohne die ursprüngliche Struktur zu stören.

Unter der Halle befindet sich ein Konferenzraum mit 100 Sitzplätzen, links und rechts von Ausstellungsflächen begleitet.

1. Section.
2. Plans (basement, ground floor, upper floor).
3, 4. Conference room.
5, 6. Owing to its marked articulation, the central
hall takes on a street-like character. This is
further accentuated by the intensive colouring,
as well as by the furnishing elements.

1. Schnitt.
2. Grundrisse (Untergeschoß, Erdgeschoß,
Obergeschoß).
3, 4. Konferenzraum.
5, 6. Die zentrale Halle hat durch ihre stark
betonte Gliederung Straßencharakter, der sowohl durch die intensive Farbgebung als auch
durch die Einrichtungselemente hervorgehoben
wird.

5

3

4

6

1, 2. Details of the scenario.
3. View from the entrance past the information desk into the customers' hall.
4. Overall view of the customers' hall, seen from the counters where air and sea travels are dealt with.

1, 2. Details des Szenariums.
3. Blick vom Eingang am Informationsschalter vorbei in die Kundenhalle.
4. Gesamtansicht der Kundenhalle von den Schaltern für Flug- und Schiffsreisen aus gesehen.

3

Sales headquarters of the Austrian Tourist Office, Vienna
Architect: Hans Hollein, assistants: Gert Michael Mayr-Keber, Franz Schönthaler, Wolfgang Schöfl and Jerzy Surwillo

The new location for the customer-orientated activities of the Austrian Tourist Office headquarters is the ground floor of the so-called Opernringhof, in particular the covered central court.

The aim of the architect was to create not only a smoothly functioning object, but also to give this object an additional dimension in keeping with the complex demands to be fulfilled which, for the most part, cannot be quantified. Consequently, the basis of the design, in addition to a comprehensive functional analysis, was the development of a scenario which would convey meanings and call up associations in many ways. To avoid having to resort to simple decoration, the medium of alienation was employed; for example, the palms signifying holidays in the South are made of brass.

The tourist office is divided into a customers' area, a clerical area with direct contact to customers, and the "hinterlands" which are aligned to the main areas but concealed from the customers.

Hauptverkaufssitz des Österreichischen Verkehrsbüros, Wien
Architekt: Hans Hollein; Mitarbeiter: Gert Michael Mayr-Keber, Franz Schönthaler, Wolfgang Schöfl und Jerzy Surwillo

Der neue Standort für die kundenbezogenen Aktivitäten der Zentrale des Österreichischen Verkehrsbüros findet sich im Erdgeschoß des sogenannten Opernringhofs und nimmt hier vor allem den zentralen überbauten Hof ein.

Es ging dem Architekten nicht nur darum, ein in seinen Abläufen gut funktionierendes Objekt zu schaffen, sondern diesem Objekt eine zusätzliche Dimension zu geben, die der Vielschichtigkeit zumeist nicht quantifizierbarer Ansprüche entspricht. Grundlage des Entwurfs war daher neben einer umfassenden Funktionsanalyse die Entwicklung eines Szenariums, das in verschiedenster Weise Bedeutungen vermittelt und Assoziationen in Gang setzt. Um dabei nicht in simple Dekoration zu verfallen, bediente man sich weitgehend des Mittels der Verfremdung; so wurden etwa die Palmen, die für Urlaub in südlichen Gefilden stehen, aus Messing gefertigt.

Organisatorisch ist das Verkehrsbüro in eine Kundenzone, eine noch im unmittelbaren Kundenkontakt stehende Bearbeitungszone und den jeweiligen Hauptbereichen zugeordnete, vom Kunden nicht einsehbare »Hinterländer« gegliedert.

1

2

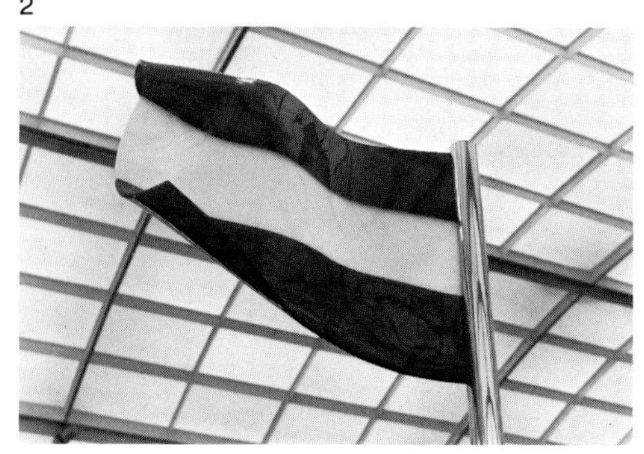

5. View past the brass palm trees towards the theatre-ticket desk with implied stage decoration.
6. Plan and section. Key: 1 entrance, 2 display, 3 information, 4 porter, 5 cash desks, 6 theatre tickets, 7 rail travels, 8 other journeys, 9 seating pavilion, 10 sea travels, 11 air travels, 12 "hinterland", 13 buffet.
7. Cashier area.

5. Blick an den Messingpalmen vorbei auf den Schalter für Theaterkarten mit angedeuteter Bühnendekoration.
6. Grundriß und Schnitt. Legende: 1 Eingang, 2 Display, 3 Information, 4 Portier, 5 Kassen, 6 Theaterkarten, 7 Bahnreisen, 8 Reisen, 9 Sitzpavillon, 10 Schiffsreisen, 11 Flugreisen, 12 »Hinterland«, 13 Buffet.
7. Kassenbereich.

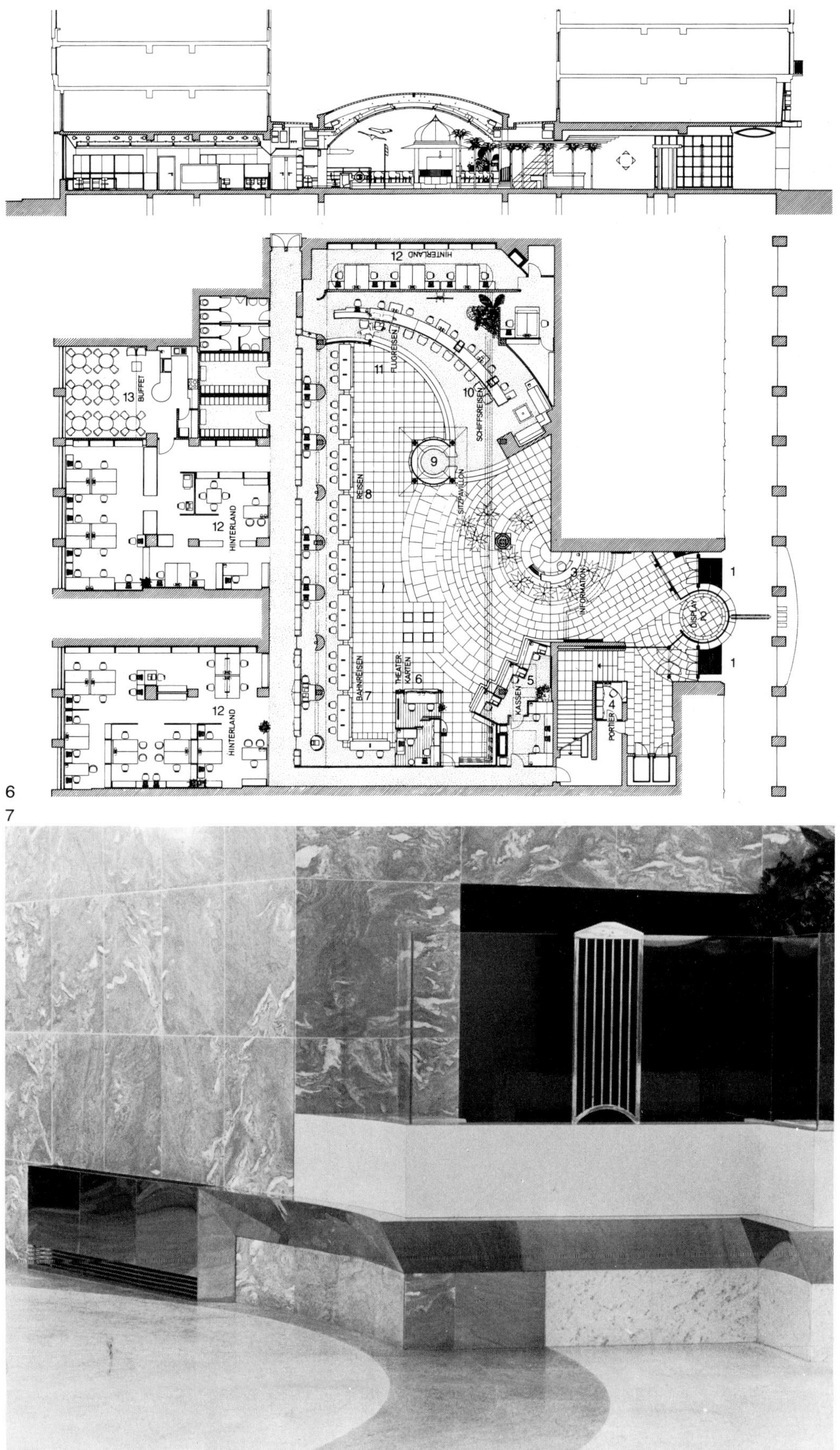

6

7

Architects/Architekten

Aalto, Alvar 104/105
Amsler, Arnold 132–135
Amsler, Vrendli 132–135
Arbeitsgemeinschaft für Architektur und
Produktgestaltung 90–93
Arbeitsgruppe für rationelles Bauen 22–24
Arnoso, Natalio 16, 17, 19, 36/37
Asseburg, Axel 108/109, 128/129
Auböck, Carl 68/69

Bayer, Herbert 14, 15, 18
Bettina, Gabriella 22–24
Bowyer, Gordon, & Partners 72–74, 80–83, 84/85
Bramante, Donato 90
Brunner, Edy 114/115
Burla, Gerd 28–31, 50/51, 130/131

Cziharz, Franz 94/95

Dierks, Frank 136–139
Dinklage, Gerd 124/125
Dranger, Jan 60/61

Ecker, Dietrich 94/95
Endell, August 12, 14, 15
Esherick, Homsey, Dodge and Davis 40/41

Feller, Ursula 22–24
Frattini, Gianfranco 70/71

Galli, Remo G. 114/115
Gandolfi, Piero 140/141
Grasberger, Helmut 124/125

Haas, Peter 16, 19, 21, 90–93
Haussmann, Robert 16, 19, 21, 47–49, 52/53,
106/107
Haussmann-Högl, Trix 16, 19, 21, 47–49, 52/53,
106/107
Hermann, Günter 16, 19, 21, 90–93
Hettig, Urs 22–24
Hollein, Hans 16, 19, 21, 75–77, 124/125,
142–145
Horta, Victor 12, 14, 15
Huber, Verena 16, 17, 19, 22–24, 25–27
Hübenbecker, Uwe 108/109
Huldt, Johan 60/61

Innovator Consult AB 60/61, 78/79
Interplay 32/33, 36/37

Jacobsen, Arne 14, 15, 18

Kammerer + Belz und Partner 13, 90
Klug, Ubald 34/35
Koerber + Hager 112/113
Kühne, Thomas 114/115
Kuramata, Shiro 14, 17, 19, 58/59, 88/89
Kuramata Design Office 56/57

Lanaro Arredamenti 126/127
Le Corbusier 14, 15, 18
Lenze, Diethelm 16, 17, 19, 32/33, 36/37
Leonori, Luca 140/141
Leonori, Tullio 140/141
Loos, Adolf 12, 15

Luz, Werner 108/109, 128/129

Mang, Eva 16, 17, 20, 96/97, 98–101, 116/117
Mang, Karl 16, 17, 20, 96/97, 98–101, 116/117
Mather, Rick, Architects 102/103
Mayr-Keber, Gert Michael 142–145
Mies van der Rohe, Ludwig 16, 17
Missoni, Herbert 94/95
MLTW/Turnbull Associates 120/121

Nelson, George, & Company 62/63

Piccaluga, Francesco + Aldo, Inc. 86/87,
110/111
Pinto, Piero 54/55, 64/65

Rabien, Helmut 128/129
Ranalli, George 16, 17, 20, 44–46
Rietveld, Gerrit Thomas 12, 15, 17
Roselius, Jobst 128/129
Rossin, Antonio 66/67

Schöfl, Wolfgang 142–145
Schönthaler, Franz 142–145
Schwarz, Fritz 122/123
Schwarz, Werner 16, 19, 21, 90–93
Singer, Helga 124/125
Steele + Bos 118/119
Stull Associates 38/39
Surwillo, Jerzy 142–145

Team A Graz 94/95
Tengblad, Magnus 60/61, 78/79
Tigerman, Stanley, and Associates 42/43

Velde, Henry van de 12, 14, 15

Wagner, Otto 10, 12, 13, 16, 17
Wallmüller, Jörg 94/95
Wallmüller, Karin 94/95
Weinbrenner, Ulrich 136–139

Sources of illustrations
Abbildungsnachweis

Alfredo Anghinelli 71 (2, 3)
Herbert Bayer/Walter Gropius/Ise Gropius, *Bauhaus 1919–1928,* 1955 18 (20)
Jeremiah O. Bragstad 40 (1, 2), 41 (4, 5), 120 (1), 121 (4, 5)
Lucca Chmel/Malina 20 (26), 96 (2), 97 (3), 98 (1, 2), 99 (4), 101 (6), 117 (3, 4, 5)
George Cserna 20 (25), 45 (2), 46 (3, 4, 5)
Thomas Cugini 122 (2, 3), 123 (4, 5)
Fridmar Damm 112 (1), 113 (3)
Robert L. Delevoy, *Victor Horta,* 1958 14 (11)
Mitsumasa Fujitsuka 19 (22), 57 (2), 58 (2), 59 (3), 89 (2, 3, 4, 5)
Johann Friedrich Geist, *Passagen. Ein Bautyp des 19. Jahrhunderts,* 1969 13 (9)
Heinz Geretsegger / Max Peintner, *Otto Wagner 1841–1918,* 1976[2] 17 (17)
Pino Guidolotti 126 (1), 127 (4, 5)
Alfred Hablützel 34 (1), 35 (2, 3, 4)
K. Hakli 104 (1, 2), 105 (3)
W. Hirsch 61 (2)
Franz Hubmann 21 (29), 75 (2), 76 (3), 124 (1), 125 (4, 5), 143 (4), 144 (5)
Greg Hursley 118 (1, 2), 119 (4)
Edgar Hyman 84 (2), 85 (3, 4, 5)
Edgar Hyman + Peter Chorley 72 (1, 2), 73 (3), 74 (5, 6), 84 (1)
Keller 136 (1), 137 (2, 3, 4), 138 (5, 6), 139 (9)
Kraufmann 13 (10)
Kraufmann u. Kraufmann 108 (1)
Le Corbusier & P. Jeanneret. Œuvre complète 1934–1938, 1953[5] 18 (19)
Karl Mang 8 (1), 9 (3), 10 (4), 11 (6), 12 (8)
Bildarchiv Foto Marburg 14 (13)
Norman McGrath 62 (1), 63 (3, 4)
F. Meyerhenn 114 (1), 115 (3)
J. P. Mieras / F. R. Yerbury, *Holländische Architektur des 20. Jahrhunderts,* 1926 17 (18)
Ludwig Münz / Gustav Künstler, *Der Architekt Adolf Loos,* 1964 15 (14, 15)
Jowa Parisini 68 (2)
Johan Pedersen, *Arkitekten Arne Jacobsen,* 1954 18 (21)
Francesco Piccaluga 86 (1, 2), 87 (4, 5), 110 (1), 111 (3, 4, 5)
Gerald Ratto 80 (1), 81 (2), 82 (4), 83 (5, 6, 7)
James Raycroft 38 (2), 39 (3, 4, 5)
Andrea Schmid 21 (27), 48 (3, 4), 49 (6)
Helga Schmidt-Glassner 12 (7)
Peter Strobel 125 (6)
Jerzy Surwillo 75 (1), 142 (1, 2, 3), 145 (7)
K. Tam 102 (1, 2), 103 (4, 5)
Friedhelm Thomas 108 (2), 109 (4, 5), 128 (1, 2), 129 (4)
Henry van de Velde, *Geschichte meines Lebens,* 1962 14 (12)
Christian Vogt 50 (1, 2), 51 (3, 4, 5, 7)
Peter Walser 21 (28), 90 (2), 91 (4), 93 (6, 7)
Museen der Stadt Wien 16 (16)
Jürg Ziegler 28 (1, 2), 29 (3, 4), 31 (8), 130 (1), 131 (3, 4)